J. S Pattinson

Far-ben

Poems in Many Moods

J. S Pattinson

Far-ben
Poems in Many Moods

ISBN/EAN: 9783337006433

Printed in Europe, USA, Canada, Australia, Japan

Cover: Foto ©Thomas Meinert / pixelio.de

More available books at **www.hansebooks.com**

FAR-BEN

OR

POEMS IN MANY MOODS

BY

J. S. PATTINSON

AUTHOR OF "CELEBRATED YORKSHIRE FOLK"

For sometimes sad, and sometimes glad,
The heart sings soft in diverse keys,
And high or low, sweet fancies flow,
The varying moods of thought to please.

LONDON:

SWAN SONNENSCHEIN & CO., LIM.

PATERNOSTER SQUARE
1899

THESE poems are dedicated to Professor A. C. BRADLEY, LL.D., Glasgow University, with grateful thanks from the Author for kind service rendered.

BRADFORD, 1899.

CONTENTS.

FAR-BEN.

Far-ben, 'tis a secret chamber
  Hid from the vulgar eye,
Where treasures of priceless value
  In thick profusion lie ;
And angels sit at the threshold,
  And mem'ry keeps the key,
And the door is always opened
  With thought of sanctity ;
For there are the dreams of childhood,
  The wonder that awoke,
When first the glory of nature
  On childish vision broke :
Who had made the glitt'ring star-land ?
  And who the radiant sun ?
And who rolled away the darkness
  When daylight was begun ?
Did God walk amid the garden
  As in Eden long ago,
And show the trees and the flowers
  The proper way to grow ?

And a thousand things since answered,
    And some not answered yet,
Lie there in that secret chamber
    Where sacred things are met.

There too are the joys of school days,
    Fair gems of priceless worth,
When the endless thirst for knowledge
    Had its first glorious birth ;
When each day disclosed some wonder,
    Each year brought more to know,
And thoughts of its boundless ranges
    Made even time seem slow.
And there the visions of youth-time
    When life's ideals sweet
Knocked gently at tender heart-strings
    And quick in pulses beat ;
When knowledge and hope were blended
    And merged in living soul,
And the future rose resplendent
    With sunshine o'er the whole,
For it held the strong endeavour,
    The purpose high and pure,
The Faith that would last for ever,
    The Love that should endure.

And there are the joys and sorrows,
    The loves of later years,

The deepest throbs of the heart-blood,
    The truest smiles and tears ;
And there are long talks at twilight,
    The fire just burning low,
And walks in a wood or meadow
    In summer's evening glow ;
And the still remembered pressure
    Left by the hand of friend,
That tells of the perfect friendship
    Which knows not stint nor end ;
And there are the woes of others
    Told for a heart relief,
And the prayers that rose with longing
    To soothe another's grief ;
And there are the falls and failures,
    And hours of long regret,
And shame for the sin and weakness
    Which chafe the spirit yet ;
And there are the books too sacred
    For common light of day,
And the golden thoughts long gathered
    Which forced the soul to pray ;
And there the hopes of the future
    Beyond our farthest ken,
When God shall take in His keeping
    The things which lie Far-ben.

THE SNOW, THE RAVEN, AND THE DROPS OF BLOOD.

'Twas through a valley wild and cold,
   As night was soft descending,
Sir Percival rode all alone
   As winter's day was ending;
Above, the sky was keen and clear,
   The stars their lamps had lighted,
And chill the frost for man and horse
   Thus in the vale benighted.

But far ahead amid the gloom
   He saw a faint light glimmer,
Then fade and die, till once again
   He caught the feeble shimmer;
And drawing to a hermit's cell
   He found the shelter needed,
Where, warmed and cheered, in slumber deep
   The night went by unheeded.

But at the dawn when forth he stepped,
   The ground with snow was covered,

And on it lay a plover, dead,
　Above, a wild hawk hovered,
Till came a raven black as night
　And drove the falcon from it,
Wheeled slowly o'er the fallen bird
　And perched and sat upon it.

While Percival looked on, thought he—
　Could I but catch the meaning,
For hidden in such scene as this
　Lies truth for human gleaning ;
The dazzling snow, the crimson blood,
　The blackness of the raven,
A picture seen a moment's space,
　But on the heart engraven.

Were Galahad but here anon,
　The snow so purely gleaming,
Would be the whiteness of the Christ,
　The blood, from cross be streaming ;
To him the raven black would be
　The symbol of some evil,
The lust of flesh, the pride of life,
　The love of self, the devil.

And Gawayne? each in his degree
　Would see his thought reflected,
Would feel an impulse, find a hope,
　Or meet a sin detected ;

Then what for me doth now appear
　　In snow of dazzling whiteness,
The glossy black of raven's wing,
　　And drops of crimson brightness?

The snow shall be her pure white skin,
　　The black her tresses flowing,
Of lady who shall henceforth be
　　The quest of all my going ;
The red shall be the crimson tide
　　Upon her cheek soft blushing,
And dropped upon her rosy lips
　　To love's perfection flushing.

Then riding swift from out the vale,
　　He passed across the meadows,
And up and down the barren hills,
　　Or in the pine tree's shadows ;
Until at length near ivied wall
　　His tardy footsteps wander ;
Perhaps, thought he, she may abide
　　In castle gleaming yonder.

So back and forth beside the stream
　　He loitered, sweetly brooding,
Till up there came a sprightly youth
　　Upon his thought intruding ;

"Thy name, Sir Knight?" he boldly said,
  "For fair thine outward seeming;"
But Percival made answer none,
  So deeply was he dreaming.

Then, lance in hand, this silent knight
  The youth would have unseated,
But from one blow he backward fell
  And found himself defeated;
Then four and twenty youths appeared,
  Each stronger than the other,
But quick and sharp beneath the blows
  They rolled on one another.

And next an older knight there came
  In angry heat of passion,
"What is thy name, and what thy quest,
  To slay men in this fashion?"
But in a trice he found himself
  Among the wounded lying,
While o'er the field in frantic haste
  His horse was wildly flying.

And then there came from castle gate
  A knight no armour wearing,
No horse to sound a swift approach,
  Nor shield nor weapon bearing;

And quick he moved across the plain
   And spoke in accents tender,
"Sir Knight," said he, "in thy distress
   What service can I render?

"For sure no man, but one distraught,
   Could work such dire confusion,
On those whose greatest crime has been
   A matter of intrusion;
Yet sure it is a churlish thing,
   From which I now am shrinking,
To come between a noble knight
   And thoughts he may be thinking."

Then Percival looked up and said,
   "My mind is constant dwelling
Upon a vision late I saw,
   And sweet past all my telling;
Of lady white as spotless snow,
   With raven hair soft flowing,
And crimson lips, like drops of blood
   Upon a snow-drift glowing.

"And when these youths so rudely came
   Between me and my dreaming,
I swept them backward, one and all,
   Of vengeance nothing deeming;

For man nor thought must come between
   My constant strong endeavour,
To find the lady of my love,
   And with her dwell for ever."

"And may thy quest," the knight replied,
   " Meet its reward full duly,
And lady white with raven hair
   Be thine to cherish truly;
But only as thy heart is pure
   And white with passion burning,
Will noblest woman's heart of love
   To thee for love be turning."

Then onward rode Sir Percival,
   By dale and hill ascending,
Or through deep valleys dark and drear
   His lonely course now wending;
But never once in castle hall,
   In glade or forest dreary,
Did he catch sight of lady fair
   For whom his heart was weary.

But often as he rode along
   He heard a voice repeating,
And from the clouds and stars it came
   In constant words of greeting,—

" But only as thy heart is pure,
   And white with passion burning,
Will noblest woman's heart of love
   To thee for love be turning."

And then the picture came again,
   Deep on his heart engraven,
The fall of snow so softly white,
   The drops of blood, the raven.
" Perchance," thought he, " I have not caught
   The fullest, truest meaning,
And richer depth of mystery
   Lies hidden for my gleaning."

Until at length by hermit's cell
   He once again alighted,
Yet once again at evening's close
   In hungry case benighted ;
And when on couch of fragrant fern
   He soon was calmly sleeping,
A vision clear as morning seen
   Was through his slumber creeping :

Upon the ground new fallen snow,
   And there the dead bird lying,
The raven sitting black as night,
   The hawk in distance flying,

And on the snow, the bright red drops
  Their tale of conflict telling,
While in the east the grey of dawn
  Was into crimson swelling.

But while he watched, the fallen bird
  Her weak wings feebly fluttered,
And quivering as with new found life,
  A plaintive cry she uttered ;
The raven rose, as through the air
  Strong golden wings are beating ;
And from afar the banished hawk
  His backward way is fleeting.

But on the snow, the wounded bird
  Her mate is gently cheering,
And tide of life, returning quick,
  Casts out all pain and fearing ;
With strength renewed by love's own balm,
  Sir Percival surprising,
She rose in air, and with her mate
  Flew towards the sun's uprising ;

While hawk and raven high above,
  Black spots of ill suspended,
Knew not to follow in the chase,
  And judged their conquest ended ;

Until at length they disappeared,
    And still the snow was lying,
With the bright drops of crimson blood
    Its clear white surface dyeing.

And Percival within his dream
    New insight was receiving,
And from across the plains of sleep
    Was deeper truth perceiving,—
" The snow is not my lady's skin,
    Nor raven black, her tresses,
The blood is not her rosy lips
    Made sweet for love's caresses ;

" For that were but to fix the heart
    On beauty's mere abstraction,
Where any sudden chance of ill
    Soon spoils the sweet perfection,
While hid beneath the outward form
    Of beauty's self external,
Lie all the greater mysteries
    Which make a love eternal.

" The snow shall be her purity,
    Her soul's own dazzling whiteness ;
Or, 'tis my honour, shows my truth,
    Sets forth my heart's uprightness ;

The drops of blood but shadow forth
  My life for her free flowing,—
Or tell her love, that so for me
  Would pour in red drops glowing;

"The hawk and raven are the ills
  From which, by my upholding,
The issues of her life shall be
  Secure in love's enfolding;
Or black and grim, they are the sins
  Of deed, or thought of lightness,
All banished, that my soul may be
  Worthy of her pure whiteness."

So passed the dream, and Percival
  Stepped forth in day's new dawning,
And breath of Spring was in the air,
  And glad the songs of morning;
And back he rode o'er vale and hill,
  And through the springing meadows,
Beside the rippling water-brooks,
  And under pine-tree's shadows;

But now, although he sought again
  The issue of his dreaming,
Across the plains, or through the glens,
  Or by some castle gleaming,

He showed a gentler courtesy
  To knight or maiden greeting,
And found each day new thought or truth
  His arc of life completing.

And when at last he found in time,
  While through a forest roving,
The lady whom his heart had sought,
  The lady of his loving,—
Her skin was white as falling snow,
  Upon the ground new lying,
Her lips like drops of crimson blood
  Its virgin whiteness dyeing.

But not like raven was her hair
  So soft and richly flowing,
But golden brown, like beechen leaves
  In the late autumn glowing;
And blue her eyes, now deep, now bright,
  Changed by each changing feeling,
And o'er her face swept rosy flush
  Her inmost thought revealing.

But whiter was her purity,
  And deep the love and tender,
That drew the heart of Percival
  Into a sweet surrender;

Yet just because his heart was pure
   And white with passion burning,
He found the woman's heart of love
   To him for love was turning.

SIR GAWAYNE AND THE GREEN KNIGHT.

GAY was the Hall, though keen round Camelot
The winds blew chill across the snowy wold.
Upon the mere no rustle mid the reeds,
Or flutter of the wild-fowl's restless wing,
And in the streams the ripples stayed themselves
In stiff'ned curves around the glassy rocks,
And mists ice cold, and fine as powdered hail,
Drove like white smoke across the shrouded land.

And cold as was the mist upon the plain
Shone Arthur's face.   In midst of gracious throng
Of knights and dames, he sat in silent state,
For when was high feast held in Camelot,
But first some bold achievement be rehearsed
Of duty done, or danger yet to come,
That so the service due to God and man
Might fall in benediction on the feast,
And make the table of the common meal

An altar of thanksgiving unto heaven
For holy task bestowed ?

Fast by his side
Upon the daïs, sat the youthful Queen,
In beauty radiant as on that spring day
When first his eye beheld her on the heights
Of troubled Cameliard ; and next to her,
With gaze intent upon the silent king,
Was Gawayne, glorious as the morning sun,
When, shooting high in heaven his golden bars,
He rises brilliant from a tideless sea
Into a cloudless sky ; yet ill at ease,
And chafing at the cause of long delay ;
For sure, he thought, it never yet hath chanced
That our brave King hath wanted stirring tale
Of action, brooding or accomplishéd,
To give him appetite.

Yet naught he spake,
And soon, with trumpet's blare, the smoking boar
Is borne aloft 'mid boughs of dusky yew ;
But, ere a guest was served, a second blast
Of silver sweetness caught the pulsing air,
And bent it backwards in o'erlapping waves,
Whose cadence, circling through the lofty Hall,
Struck to each heart a wild expectant thrill
Of great adventure soon to be fulfilled ;

And as each knight caught all unconsciously
At jewelled hilt amid his silken scarf,
And half uprose to guard he scarce knew what,
The doors swung open as by magic touch,
And, bending low, to clear the lintel bar,
There entered knight, as ne'er before or since
Had graced the lists of far-famed Camelot ;—
For green as meadows in the early spring
His hose and jerkin, free from armour dight,
And green his steed and trappings, bit and bell
And bridle, hoof and mane.   One massive hand
Waved overhead a branch of holly, specked
With blood-drops, while the other grasped an axe
With mystic symbols wrought ; and where the haft
And trenchant blade found union, was a band
Of fine-cut emeralds, which caught the lights
Of torch and taper, and then flashed them back
In long and slender lines of piercing green
Across the faces of the guests, till each
Became unreal as a fading dream.

Huge as a giant from the fabled lands
Beyond Arcturus was the stranger knight,
And huge his steed,—yet never sound of bit
Or harness broke on startled ear : no noise
Of answering foot-fall from the pavement rose,
As swift the green hoofs cleared the narrow space
And paused before the daïs of the King ;

When, rising in his seat, the Green Knight swung
His axe in menace at the gazing throng,
And cried aloud, "Come one, your bravest, best;
Let strike who may, I will abide the stroke;
But this year and a day, come fair, come foul,
Within the secret of my Chapel Green
Must I return the blow. What, silent still?
Then true it is that all your valiant deeds
Are fables, and your prowess boastful words;
Your king a changeling, good for such as ye,
Who boast, yet fear to meet a worthy foe."

Whereat the King, the crimson tide of wrath
Scorching like flame the whiteness of his face,
Upstarting, stretched an eager hand, and cried,
"Have here thine axe, and by the God of Heaven
Thine head shall pay the scandal of thy tongue!"
But as the knight leaped lightly from his steed,
Sir Gawayne, swifter, knelt at Arthur's feet
And said: "A boon, my Lord the King! Ah not
For thee to prove thy knighthood on this knave,
Or wipe the insult from our Order true;
Thou,—who hast won in battle sore and long
A fame outlasting as the farthest tides
Of vast humanity. Then grant to me,
Who am the youngest, and the feeblest here
Of all thy hundred fifty chosen knights,
And whose one claim to honour lies alone

In kinship unto thee,—grant me, I pray,
This conflict strange to wage, since losing thee,
The kingdom loseth all, but by my loss
Scarce poorer will it prove."

Cold bowed the King,
And axe in hand, and head thrown firmly back,
Stood Gawayne forth, the flower of all the court,
Ere yet the heat of passion, darkening down
To evening, cast long shadows black and gaunt
Athwart the troubled land ; and grimly smiled
The giant knight, as stooping low, he bent
His neck to bear the stroke.
                     Aloft the axe
Shot like a lightning flash through the still air,
Then fell with sweep so clean, that far the head
Rolled o'er the floor, spurned by the dainty foot
Of loudly cheering guest : while from the trunk,
Which now stood upright as before the stroke,
The dark blood leaped, a thick and gurgling fount,
That flowed across the pavement of the Hall
A purple stream, yet left no stain or spot
On tunic or on hose.

                     But the Green Knight,
Uplifting in his hand the severed head,
The hair and beard bedabbled all with gore,
Sprang to the saddle, caught the bridle rein,

And as the steed reared ready to be gone,
The eyelids lifted, and the red fierce eyes
Rolled lurid flame, and from the parted lips
There rang the fateful words — "Well struck, Sir
    Knight!
A right man should so goodly stripling prove.
Sir Gawayne, art thou?   Heed thy promise then,
To seek me hence a year and but a day,
When in the Chapel Green I will not fail
To give thee full requital for thy blow;
Till then, Farewell."   And bounding madly forth
With head in hand, the Green Knight flashed from
    sight,
The hoofs struck lightnings 'neath their silent blows,
And once again a long and piercing blast
From silver trumpet echoed through the Hall,
As knights all speechless each on other gazed,
And knew not if they dreamed, or if they woke,
Or if they lived indeed.

          At length the King,
Recovered from the spell, commands the axe
Be hung above his throne, and that the feast
Proceed with mirth and song; "For now," quoth he,
"Our soul is satisfied.   It is ill done
Were we to think on meats, and pass the cup,
And feast like heathen, while that part divine
Which strives within us, is the life of God,

Goes hungry, lean, and cold.   And thou, young sir,
My sister's son, have double portion served,
And Jesu grant thee grace, the worser half
Of thine adventure to fulfil."

Never, since life began, had year revolved
So slowly from its prime to dreary close,
As now to Gawayne passed the months and days.
Before the west wind and the climbing sun
The frost king fled, and once again was heard
The music of the brooklet, and the fall
Of deep brown waters far amid the rocks ;
And from beneath the shroud of melting snow
The land burst forth in robe of living green,
And through the glades the cuckoo sang to greet
The resurrection of another spring.
The daffodil and slender wind-flower waved
Their last pale petals over primrose paths,
And late forget-me-nots blushed rosy pink,
Then faded out before the foxglove blooms ;
The hawthorn fell in showers of scented snow
Across the hyacinth plains of dusky blue,
And grasses, sweet with clover, wooed the bee,
And sheltered beast and bird and creeping thing,—
While thrush and blackbird sang the dawn of love,
Its consummation, saw their young ones fly
To sing as sweet in the succeeding year ;—
So spring to summer wound its wonted way,

And summer deepened into autumn glow,
And faster coursed the blood within his veins,
As Gawayne watched the skies grow red at eve,
And saw the bracken golden on the hills ;
When burned the second glory of the gorse,
And the red maple turned the woods to fire
Beneath the yellow gleam of chestnut fans ;
And all the fields with crimson colour hedged
Of hip, and haw, and trailing briony,
Were soft and sweet with luscious after-grass,—
For now across the stubbly corn-lands lay
The pathway of his promise, where afar
He must abide the conflict, life or death,
Within the Chapel Green.

        So came at last
All Hallow's Day, when, at the parting feast
In Arthur's Hall, great cheer was made for him.
And on the morrow, bright as mid-day sun,
He knelt in golden armour, while the priest
Breathed blessings o'er him; and fair maidens brought
His helmet richly decked, and girt his sword
About him with a scarf of deep-toned blue,
And armed him with a mystic shield, enwrought
On one side with a gold pent-angle, clear
On field of crimson, while on the reverse
The virgin Mother held aloft a crown
In which five virtues burned in starry points,

Frankness, Fidelity, and Purity,
And Courtesy with Pity, and in each
There glowed a heart of crimson, pulsing still
From the five wounds of Christ.

           Then, waiting, stood
Before the door, his charger Gringolet,
On whose fair neck the King laid gentle hand,
And turned to Gawayne with regretful sigh,—
"Ah, happy youth, thy life an ardent spring,
As yet unscorched by summer's blist'ring sun,
My heart could envy thee the first mad joy
Of maiden exploit in an unknown land.
But to each season, to each span of years,
Is given a task of glory all its own.
'Tis thine to prove thine armour, still undimmed
By stress of mortal combat : mine to wage
A war familiar grown, and so beset
With peril, lest the future shame the past ;
Lest I should fail to find my highest crown
Amid the evening shadows, ere I go."

Strange were the lands through which Sir Gawayne
      now
Rode onward to his quest. By mountain pass,
And over wide waste plains, where the dry heath
Sighed dirge-like in the low and dead'ning wind,
And where the last flags of the cotton grass

Waved ragged in a sea of brown and grey.
And as the days grew shorter, and the sun
Scarce rose above the topmost ridge of rock,
He passed by waters wan and chill as death,
And in the night the sleet and driving snow
Froze in his hair; and from the forest black
Came the fierce howling of the famished wolves,
And timid foxes shot across his path,
Until on Christmas Eve, full sore bespent,—
He turned, to where, beyond the naked trunks,
A streak of red ran straight athwart the sky,
And rearing up his shield, now heavy grown,
Against a tree, he knelt with head bent low,
And prayed, "Oh Thou who didst within Thine heart
The sorrows of Thy Son so meekly share,
Pity my weakness, grant my last request,—
To hear, when breaks again the advent morn,
The matin bell, and through the Holy Mass
To pass far hence to distant Avalon,
Or, void of light and hope, an outcast lost,
I die as heathen in a heathen land."

     Scarce had he crossed himself
When on a height, within the sunset's glow,
A lustrous castle stood ; and as a dream
The forest faded, and behold a park,
In grassy undulations, swept to where
A moat wound round the massy wall, and girt

C

The rocky base.   Then was Sir Gawayne glad ;
And seizing fast his pommel, dragged his limbs
Across the green, when to his feeble call
A porter answered from beyond the moat,
And asked his name and will.

                       "Gawayne, my name,
My need, a shelter from the winter frost,
That so, renewed in strength, I still may seek
And find the Knight of the famed Chapel Green,
In this or other land."

                       With that the bridge
Was lowered quick, and up the pathway steep,
Which wound in circles round the giant rock,
Went Gawayne, till in midmost of a Hall,
Bright as the loved and distant Camelot,
Kind faces thronged, and warm and gentle hands
Stripped off his armour, led him softly forth,
Bathed his stiff limbs, and clothed him courteously
In silken robe, fine wrought with threads of gold,
And shoes of varied hue ; and brought him straight
To where in ivied hall the baron kept
The Yule-tide feast.   And Gawayne, now renewed
In strength and courage, spoke in lightsome tone
Of his adventures through the wintry land,
And told his promise to the huge Green Knight,
To meet him on the advent of the year
Within his Chapel Green.

At this the Lord
Laughed loud and long. "Ah ha! Sir Knight,"
   said he,
"So thou art bound upon that fatal quest
Which many a better man than thou hast rued?
But tarry here, our Yule-tide feast we keep,
And for three days the stranger, high or low,
Is honoured guest, at bed and board and song,
For the sweet Christ, His sake." With that the feast,
Enhanced by kindness wrought, went merrily
Till far into the night; and oft the dame,
The Lady of the castle, where she sat
Beside her Lord, cast ling'ring looks of love
On Gawayne, which forsooth he heeded not,
Nor knew that thus he fanned the growing flame,
And stirred a keen desire within her breast
To mould him to her will.

    So three days passed
With revelry, then came the Feast of John,
When all the guests, with ample largesse given,
And courteous thanks, rode from the castle gate.
But the bluff Lord, when Gawayne would depart,
Prayed that he still would tarry three days' space.
"Thy long-sought goal is scarce three miles away,
And thou shalt have a stout and trusty guide
To do thee service due. But I myself
Must ride each morning to the distant hunt,

Within the forests dark'ning towards the north,
While thou shalt bide in the sweet company
Of my fair dame, and make her goodly cheer,
And each at nightfall shall to other give
What gifts the day may bring."

           The bargain struck,
The Baron, as each evening fell, bestowed
Upon his guest fat deer, and grisly boar,
And ruddy fox in turn.   While the young knight,
As crept the hours, longed for the open plain,
And oft-times gazed across the grassy slopes
Which lay so fair beneath the winter sun,
And yearned to feel once more between his knees
The heaving sides of his good Gringolet,
And see the landscape pass, and know himself
Clad as befits a knight : for through the day
Strange fancies seized him in the sun-lit hall,
And in the Lady's bower.   And oft it seemed
That airy forms bent round him, breathed his name,
Then melted from him in a warm embrace ;
And kisses, light and soft as rose-leaf dropped
By summer wind, fell on his boyish lips.
And waking in the early morn, he saw
The Lady glide across his chamber floor,
And heard the rustle of her silken robes,
As on the threshold her light foot-step stayed,
And then the ripple of her laughter sweet,

As ling'ringly the foot-falls passed away
And died upon his ear.   And oft she spoke
To him of love, toyed with his silken hair,
And wooed him with the languor of her eyes ;
And then she wept her own unhappy fate
Which bound her to a Lord too old for love,
And bent upon the chase.
                 But Gawayne, strong
In the one purpose of his sacred quest,
Unmoved and cold, returned no fond caress,
And ever as there loomed before his sight
The coming conflict, fast aside he threw
Each foul temptation, crushed the rising thought,
Ere it had formed itself into a wish
To stain his spotless soul ; and day by day,
The kisses which against his word and will
The dame bestowed, he paid most faithfully
At night-fall to the Baron, as agreed,
For booty of the hunt.

                But on the third,
The final day, the love-lorn lady clung
Around him weeping sore.   "Alas," said she,
"That one so young should scorn delight of love,
And court grim death in that far valley dread
Where stands the Chapel Green.   But an thou must,
Take then this ring of gold, and for my sake
Wear it throughout the fight, that so thy foe

May see thee compassed round by am'rous thought,
And know that some fair lady prays for thee
To ease thy path to death."
                        But when he spoke
No word of thanks, nor took the proffered ring,
She murmured low, " Bethink thee, gentle youth,
With hair as bright as gleam of sunshine cast
On the bent swathe of fully-ripened corn,
And skin soft as the hue of guelder-rose,
When the long glow of summer sun-set skies
Flushes the petals to an answ'ring blush
In the sweet month of June ;—bethink thee, youth,
That certain death awaits thy foolish quest,—
And death is cold, its touch is ghastly, grim,
To men far spent upon the way of life,
And weary with its pain ; but what for thee,
Within whose veins the young blood courses hot,
And to whose azure eye one half the sights
And pleasures of this fair and sensuous world
Have not revealed themselves ?   Oh, save thyself!
Take thou this jewelled belt, set thick with gems
Enwoven in a band of emerald green,
Which worn beneath thine armour will preserve
Thee from all danger, stay the stroke of death,
And save thee from thy fate."
                        When thus she spoke
Of death, an icy chill crept to his heart,
And all his rich and warmly-pulsing blood

Seemed turned to water for a moment's space,
His courage wavered, and, when evening fell,
Sir Gawayne gave the kisses as before,
But kept the magic belt.

The next day broke
In gloom, and fog, and sheets of driving snow ;
But as the cock crew in the dismal morn,
Sir Gawayne leaped from out his sleepless bed,
Buckled his golden armour by the light
Of a small lamp, while round his waist was wound
The lady's girdle ; took his helm and shield,
And mounted once again on Gringolet,
Whose glossy sides betokened ample care,
With thanks to Lord and menial, forth he rode
In storm and fog, and o'er the dreary plain
There followed close an ancient serving man
To bear his lance and spear.

But when afar,
'Mid rocks half hidden in the drifted snow,
They reached the base of a steep, rugged hill,
From which a valley, dark with haunting shades,
Wound into deeper gloom, the old man paused,—
"Ah, good Sir Knight," said he, " be warned in time,
And hie thee back ere death thy way o'ertake ;
For never any—noble, monk, or priest—
Hath ere returned from that dread Chapel Green,

Which now thou seekest to thy deadly hurt.
Then turn thee, turn thee to thine own fair land,
Where fame and lady's love for thee await,
And never shall one word of mine betray
Thy secret, or assoil thy name."

                    At this,
Sir Gawayne, all his face aflame, and hot
With anger, started forward at quick pace,
Then checked himself to answer courteously :—
" I ride, come weal, come woe, with heart intent
Upon fulfilment of a promise due.
Come life, with foul dishonour in its prime,
The stolen years will be a living death.
Come death with honour, and my name shall live
In noble impulse to the Table Round,
While I shall pass along the seven-hued bridge
To that most beauteous land of Avalon,
Where courage beats in every pulse of air,
And failure never falls."

                " Have, then, thy lance,
And Heaven protect thy head !"   So the old man
Turned homeward through the fog ; and Gawayne
        rode
Alone into the dark and loathsome vale,
Where deep green pools lay sheer across his path,
And black frost dripped from bare and twisted boughs

Of blasted trees, whose creaking branches waved,
Although no wind passed by.
         At length he paused
Beside a stream, whose murky surface boiled
In oily bubbles round the shiny rocks, —
For on the bank a rounded hill uprose,
Untouched by frost; green as when April suns
Glint radiant colour through the passing showers.
Beneath, around, black winter, drifts of snow
Grey in the gloomy fog ; but here was spring,
And Gawayne marvelled, while across the stream,
From far beyond the dark and leafless trees
There came, then ceased, then ever came again,
A low weird sound, like wind among the pines
Which crown some distant hill,—a sound which crept,
He knew not why, in surging waves of chill
And icy horror through his frame, that stayed
His blood for a brief moment's space, that froze
His hand upon the rein, and seemed to turn
His hair to icicles beneath his helm ;—
" Surely," thought he, " this place is meetlier far
For devil to say mass at midnight hour,
Than for a Christian knight to keep his tryst
And match him with his foe."

         But as his blood
Returned in warm and living flow, he sprang
From off his steed, and round the nearest branch

Of a bare linden tree he threw the rein,
And finding three low entrances, he passed
Within the hill,—but it was hollow all,
And dank with fungus; and the oozy slime
Dropt from the sides, and crept along the floor
In slow grey streams, and bats with angry wing
Beat round him in the dusk.

     Then out again
Beside the oily stream, he stood and cried,
" Is none in this strange land, in this dark vale,
To have discourse with me?   If such an one
Hear now my words, let him come hither straight ;
I wait his wish and will ! "
       But no reply
Came to him through the thick and heavy air,
Save that the sound from far across the stream
Came nigher, and he knew it for the whirr
Of grindstone, and the sharpening of an axe.
Yet still a second time did Gawayne cry
On unseen foe, when from the further bank
Came the one word, "Abide !" And sparks arose
Behind some blighted laurel trees, and swift
And louder whirred the grinding stone, then ceased,
Or passed in laughter.
      "Ay, abide, Sir Knight,
And thou shalt have, perchance too soon, who knows,
That which I promised thee !"   And with the words

The Green Knight leaped the gurgling, turbid stream,
And leaning on his axe, whose broad clean blade
Shone brilliant 'mid the gloom,—
        "Welcome!" he cried,
"Sir Gawayne, for thou well hast kept thy pledge
To meet me here. But, peradventure, now
Thy heart doth fail at thought of deadly stroke;
And so that be, then hie thee hence away,
Mine axe is sharp and sure."

        The hot blood leaped
To Gawayne's face, as swift he doffed his helm
And threw it 'midst the rocks. Then bending down
His head, he cried, "Strike on, good knight,
For had I feared thee or thy doughty blow
I had not sought thee through the winter storms,
And all the ghostly horrors of this land."
Then high the axe whizzed through the murky air,
And at the eerie swish, there crept once more
To Gawayne's heart the fear that made him quail
Within the Lady's bower, and chilled his blood
At sharp'ning of the axe; and a cold sweat
Broke over him, and slight his shoulders shrank
As scarce to move the muscles of his neck,
Or slack the grip of hands upon his knees,
But the axe dropped, as the Green Knight exclaimed
"A coward art thou? Dost thou fear to lose
Some lady's love? Or art thou loath to spoil

Those golden locks with thy white craven blood?
A knight indeed !   Ay, when the stroke is thine,
And mine the head to fall.   Go hence, I say,
Thou art not worth the shine and sharp'ned edge
Of my new Danish blade."

                    But Gawayne stirred
Nor head, nor hand, nor foot, while the black fog
Grew deeper in the glen.
                    " What, anxious still
To test the strength of thy too boastful words?"
And once again the axe was raised, but stayed
As sudden in its sweep, while the Green Knight
Approached the youth, and swept the clust'ring curls
From off his fair white neck.
                    "'Tis better so,
Thy head will be a gift the choicer far
To greet my lady, with these golden locks
To show thou wast a man most passing fair,
Although of coward heart."   And stepping back
He swung the axe the third time far aloft,
And as it fell with a shrill piercing scream,
Sir Gawayne motionless, his armour dim,
His silken scarf low drooping on the ground,
And Gringolet soft calling in his ear
With gentle whinny, as she pawed the snow,
Had passed the gates of death :—for swifter far
Than was the sweep of axe through yielding air,

There rose before him the gay lighted hall
In distant Camelot, and o'er a bier,
On which there lay the body of a knight,
With golden hair, and armour stained with blood,
And on his breast a shield, whereon were seen
The bleeding wounds of Christ, the God-like King
Waved hands of benediction, while his face
Shone with a beauty whose deep inward source
Was joy of noble deed not wrought by him,
But by the impulse of his soul inspired,
And wrought for love of him.   " So pray I God
That every knight be perfect, true to death,
His soul white, not as in his childhood's days
Of guileless innocence, but through the fire
Of trial purified ; " and as there burst
Through the wide hall a loud triumphant song,
The blow descending fell with touch so soft
As scarce to break the skin.
            But as the blood
Fell in few drops upon the trampled snow,
Sir Gawayne sprang, and seizing lance and shield
Cried joyously, " So is the compact o'er !
One stroke alone was thine.   Now hilt to hilt
We wage an equal war, save that to thee
Advantage falls of height, and strength of limb."

But the Green Knight stood smiling kindly down
On his small rage, as tow'ring hill might smile

Upon the wind-tossed lakelet at its base,
And from his lips there came in accents sweet
Strong words of peace: "Gawayne, put up thy sword,
The victory is thine. Thou gavest me
Each night the kisses which, throughout the day,
My wife bestowed on thee, for 'twas my will
That thou shouldst prove thy virtue in the fire
Of strong temptation, and seductful words,
All set to urge thy fall. That thou didst shrink
From the first blow, it was the magic power
Of that green girdle clasped around thy waist,
Which thou didst cherish, but the which is mine,
And called the 'Fear of Death.' That is atoned
By these red drops of life. And now depart,
A knight in virtue perfect ; white thy soul
As yonder cloudlets breaking in the west,
And never more shall coward fear of death
Unnerve thine arm, or bid thy courage fail ;
For thou hast conquered that last enemy
Which steals the souls of men from high emprise,
And sets the life, which might have scaled the heights
Of noblest purpose, in some valley dread
Of chilling frost and fog."

　　　　　　As Gawayne watched,
The Green Knight turned to semblance of his host,
Then faded from his view. The sun burst forth,
And lo the land was green ; the stream which late

Had boiled in oily bubbles at his feet
Now gently tinkled in a pebbly bed ;
A lark sang clear and strong, and softly white
The clouds sailed swan-like in an azure sky ;
And fast as Gawayne rode, the grass sprang sweet
And dewy 'neath his charger's feet, and flowers
Bloomed by the wayside, and the peasant folk,
As swift he passed in beauty from their sight,
Gazed upward to the sun-lit arch of Heaven,
And crossed themselves for joy, that now the Spring
Was breaking o'er the land.

THE LADY OF THE FOUNTAIN.

"TELL us a tale!"

                 And Guinivere looked full
At Kynon, where he sat beside the frame,
In which the small hand of Ymoneth wove
A pattern wrought in gold, on groundwork blue
As were her own sweet eyes.

                    For Arthur, spent
With following of the chase, slept in his seat
Of fragrant rushes, over which was cast
A robe of amber silk ; and in the light
Of the wide window were fair maidens, some
Intent upon the silken tracery
Of bird and leaf and flower, and some intent
On the broad landscape, as it rolled in green,
To where a rugged line of purple hills
Shut in the summer sky.

               But at the words
All eyes glanced bright and quick at Kynon first,
Then passed to Ewayne, where he lounged beside
The low couch of the Queen.   But Ewayne blushed

And shook his head in fear, for he was shy
In ladies' company ; while Kynon smiled,
And rising straight, bowed low in courtesy,
And leaning 'gainst a pillar, with the free
And easy grace which knows itself for grace,
And toying with the crimson scarf, which hung
In silken folds down to his broidered shoes, —
" Fair Lady," quoth he, " will it please your ear,
If I should tell of an adventure strange
Late happened to myself ? "

      " Nay," said the Queen,
" The hero will enchance the deeds." While some
Of the young maidens smiled a curious smile,
And Ewayne murmured, " Of himself forsooth ! "

But Kynon noted not, so full he was
Of pleasing thoughts about himself, and how
His skill could now be shown.

     " So please your Grace,
'Tis but a story of a recent quest
To find a man in every knightly sport
More mighty than myself ; for of a truth,
'Tis known in court that none more brave
Than I doth wield a sword, or couch a spear,
Or—tell a pleasant tale.

     "And so it chanced,
That riding forth one day in early June,

D

I happened on a valley, which the like
For beauty I had never seen before,—
For snowy hawthorn whitened every hedge,
And high above there drooped a shower of gold
From the slim branches of laburnum trees,
And chestnut boughs flamed their tall tapers forth,
And, scattered on the grass, the tinted blooms
Of apple orchards, and the fairy spray
From the wild cherry cast.   And on the hills
Fawns glanced between the thick and rounded stems
Of oak and sycamore, while through the vale
A river, deep, and lovelier than the Usk,
Washed the bare roots of low-set willow trees,
And murmured soft beneath the darker shades
Of heavy alder boughs ; and on the banks
The iris blue as heaven, or like the flame
Of some tall candle yellow in the sun ;
And by the river a long winding path,
The which I took, and travelled through the heat
Of mid-day, and the radiant afternoon,
Till in the evening wide before me lay
An open plain, in midst of which there shone
A lustrous castle, and beside the gate
A fountain silver as an Easter moon
When all the sky is clear.

        "Close to the fount,
Two youths, in purple tunics fringed with gold,

And bound with golden belts ; with leather shoes
Of rainbow colours, clasped with boss of gold,
And hose of purple silk,—through the fine spray
Shot long white arrows tipped with gold, and winged
With peacock's feathers ; while beside them stood
A man, not young, nor old, with close-cut beard,
Who wore a robe of yellow satin slashed
With silver points, and bound about the waist
With a thick silver coil, and hung therefrom
Were silver tassels set with amethysts,—
Who straight saluted me, and bade me come
To his fair castle, where the evening meal
Awaited but the guest.

   " And fair indeed
The castle and the hall ; and waiting there
Were four and twenty maidens, each one tall
And lovely as a dream, whene'er the dream
Is hallowed by a vision sweet of thee ; "
And here he bowed to the attentive Queen ;
While from the low and sunny window seat
Ymoneth glanced from an acanthus scroll,
And frowned in pretty scorn ;—

   " For six were dark,
With hair like raven's wing, and eyes as black
As sloes in autumn, who without a word
Led forth my steed ; and six, with rosy flush,

And bright red lips, and hair of rippling brown,
Took my soiled armour to remove the stains ;
And six, with dazzling skin, and auburn hair
Touched with a gleam of gold, bathed my tired limbs,
Combed my rough locks, and clad me in a robe
Of sumptuous colours ; while the other six,
Whose tresses shamed the wondrous fair cocoon
The silk-worm weaves far in the sunny south,
And whose blue eyes were like the speedwell flower,
With airy motion passed through the long hall
With divers meats, and fruits in golden bowls,
And brought rare wines in goblets white and red,
And set them forth, a tempting rich array,
Upon a silver table, where it stood
In midmost of the hall.

      " But never word
Was spoken till the meal was wholly done,
And then the host enquiring of my quest,
I told him how I journeyed far and wide
To find the man in tilt or tournament
Should throw me in fair fight.
       " 'Then thou hast come
Unto the right and proper land,' quoth he ;
'And if to-morrow morn thou take thy way
Through the thick beechwood at the valley's head,
Until within a glade a mound appear,
And on the mound, a man both tall and great,

Seated upon a stone.   No comely sight
To gaze upon ; for but one eye he hath,
And that in midmost of his forehead set ;
And lame he is, and in his hand he bears
An iron club, for he is Wood-ward there,
And round him throng the timid forest things
That shun the haunts of men : Ask thou of him
And he will straight direct thy simple quest.'

"So, in the morn, 1 rode through beechen wood
Unto the glade, and found as had been told,
Save that no beast appeared ; but at my wish
The one-eyed man smote with his iron club
A solitary stag, and at its cry,
Came crowds of deer, and goats, and timid hares,
As thick as stars on a clear frosty night,
And serpents green and black, and dragons fierce,
Till scarce there was the space for me to stand ;
And when the man, with one hand held aloft,
Breathed forth the words, ' Beloved, now depart !'
They bowed their heads in answer, and forthwith
Passed out from sight, but feeding as they went.

"Then in my heart arose a wave of fear
Of this strange forester ; but when I told
The object of my quest, he bade me now
Return along the glade, and climb a path
Which led straight upward o'er a wooded hill

Until a valley opened wide and bare,
With, in the centre, one tall spreading tree,
Greener than any pine, and 'neath its shade
A fountain, with a marble slab hard by,
And silver bowl thereon.
     " 'Take thou the bowl,
And fill it from the fountain ; o'er the slab
Dash thou the water, and anon will burst
Such peal of thunder as ne'er shook, I trow,
The Hall of thy great King ; and then shall fall
A shower of hail so fierce, that hardly wilt
Thou 'scape from it alive ; and after that
Soft music such as mortal ear ne'er heard
Shall break from myriad birds ; and through the vale
Will meet thee sable knight on sable steed,
Black as the deepest cave of dismal death,—
Of him ask combat, and I promise thee
Thou shalt be left at closing of the fray
Horseless upon the plain !'

     " And so, fair Queen,
All happened as he said,
      " For scarce the sun
Had tipped the purple hills, when forth I rode
Through the long flowery glade, and up the hill,
Till far below me spread a barren vale,
In 'midst, the single tree.   Then with the bowl
I dipped the water from the fountain clear

And dashed it o'er the slab, when instantly
Crash went the sky, the very air was burst
Asunder with the shock, the solid earth
Was looser than a quagmire to my feet,
And ere the trembling ceased, hail like to darts
Fell through the broken air, which on my shield
I caught (the marks remain to test my truth),
Else had they pierced me through, and cut their way
Deep to the very bone.

      " But when the hail
Had ceased to fall, the tree was leafless, bare
As when mid-winter winds sigh o'er the land ;
While to the south a gentle murmur rose,
First a complaining sound, like distant sea
When low it frets against some rocky cliff ;
And next the chant of an advancing choir,
And then a burst of choral harmony,
As all the air grew dark with flocks of birds,
Who perched in the bare branches overhead,—
And which was thrush, or which was nightingale,
I thought not, for that each distinctive note
Was lost in music, and I thereby ceased
To think at all.
      " But while entranced I stood,
There rode towards me on his sable steed
The knight in armour black as dismal death,
And black his lance and shield. With angry eye

He glared upon me as I stood beneath
The bare and blasted tree.
                    "'Good sir !' he cried,
'What evil have I done that thou shouldst blast
My land with tempest, and my fields with hail ?
No beast is left to wander through my woods,
No leaves hang on my trees ; my land is reft
Of every living thing, and winter drear
Reigns on this summer day ; prepare thee then
To prove thy right to enter my domain,
Or pay the price of thy temerity.'

"With that we each at other rode, and fast
The sods flew upward 'neath our horses' feet,
And thrice methought he must have dropped before
The vigour of my lance.
                    "But he was strong,
And heavy, and of monstrous size to boot,
And so, to end my tale, he threw me quite,
Passed his long lance within my bridle rein,
And riding off, as my strange friend foretold,
I found myself at closing of the fray
Horseless upon the field.

                    "With lagging steps
I to the castle dragged my weary way ;
But as I left the vale, methought I heard
A low soft wailing,—'twas perhaps the wind
Amid the leafless branches overhead,—

But yet it followed me, till in the Hall
I lost it midst the welcome ministries
Of the young maidens, who, no questions asked,
Anointed me with fragrant oils, and cheered
My heart with wine, and in the morning brought
Fresh horse and arms, and bade a kind farewell.
Then home I rode beneath the hawthorn trees,
And first to thee, fair Queen, have I rehearsed
This fruitless quest of mine."

       When Kynon ceased
A varied murmur rose.   Some praised his tale,
While others thought it wanted point, or aim,
Since naught had been achieved ; and of them all
Ymoneth spoke no word, though Kynon watched
For lifting of the golden head which bent
Above the golden scroll.
       " And so, Sir Knight,
On ventures such as these ye ride abroad,"
Laughed the young Queen.   " Well, 'tis a pretty tale,
In harmony with summer afternoon
Of drowsy loveliness."
       But Ewayne sprang
From the low rug beside the silken couch,
And casting off the shyness, which on him
Was mantle that concealed a fervent will,
He stood before them with his face aflame,
And eyes which shot steel lightnings from the blue,

And in his voice there rang the undertone
Of what the issues of his life would be
In the far future years.

          " And dost thou boast
Of failure, thou, a knight of Camelot ?
Methinks it is indeed a pretty tale,
And sweetly told forsooth.   But what good knight
Would leave oppression unrelieved, and, spent
Or weary, save himself, if sigh of woe
Fell ever on his ear ?

          " Not ended, no,
Not ended was thy task, when the Black Knight
O'erthrew thee on the plain ; nay, for in truth
It was but just begun.   Although unhorsed
And beaten in the strife, 'twas surely thine,
Though death had been the guerdon, to pursue
Thy quest, and listening to those murmurs strange
'Twas thine to free the land from blighting curse,
And not to seek thy safety and thine ease
In such unknightly fashion as thou say'st."

But Kynon flushed with anger, tossed his head,
And cried, "Go thou, my friend ! and when unhorsed,
With broken lance, and limbs all bruised and sore,
Prove thou thy knighthood on that foul black knave,
And I will give thee leave to reckon me
A coward, or assoil my name ; but not,
Good sir, till then."

At this the King awoke,
And asked the cause of discord in the Hall ;
And when the story of the fruitless quest
Was quick rehearsed to him by Guinivere,
He looked at Ewayne with admiring glance,
But spoke reprovingly.

"Be not in haste
To judge a seeming fault. The many men
In many ways attain their noblest selves.
Some, long before the dawn of manhood, find
Their souls attuned to duty, and their wills
Subdued to perfect self-control,—and such
Art thou, Sir Ewayne.

"Others need the lapse
Of moments fraught with pain, and hours of shame,
When conscience waves her burning torch amid
Fair conquests left unsought, or glory lost,
When the whole man, recoiling at the sight,
Turns with a cry to meet his better self
In pure ideals, seen but unattained,
And through the shame of this his lower life,
And by the vision of the might-have-been,
He rises ere the days become too late
To noble doing in a noble cause :—
And thus may Kynon fare."

"And that, my King,
Before yon swiftly west'ring sun has set.

For truth to tell, those piteous moans have oft
Disturbed my soul, when most serene appeared
The outer semblance of my late content.
And oft when slumber held aloof, and left
My mind twice open to the unseen world,
Have those same murmurs chased the idle thoughts
With which I strove in vain to fill my soul,
And daily have I known myself the worser man,
Because I saw the task I would not do,
Because I heard the call I would not heed,
And felt the impulse, but withheld the will.
Lead on, Sir Ewayne, thou the better knight,
And I will follow thee, thy squire, thy slave,
And never shall these Halls behold me more,
Till I have wiped from off my tarnished shield
That dread black stain of shame."
              And as he spoke,
He saw the golden head, no longer bent
Over acanthus scroll, but turned to him ;
And from the eyes, now dark and deeply blue
As tarns hid far between the misty hills,
There came a beam of light, in which he saw
Himself transfigured to her highest wish
And purpose for his life ; and taking up
A strand of silk as golden as her hair,
He tied it loosely in his crimson scarf,
And whispered in a strange and earnest tone
" Ymoneth, when to-morrow I ride forth

With thy young brother on this nobler quest,
Upon my helmet will this strand be seen,
And never shall thine eyes behold my face
Till I deserve that they shall look on me
With glow of pride, as now with glow of love,
They burn into my soul."

   In the new morn,
When the long level bars of crimson light
Broke into yellow beams, then intermixed,
And rose a flood of orange glory cast
On the far dusky hills, the castle gate
Was busy as the noon ; and from the tide
Of fond farewells, and wishes fraught with love,
Sir Ewayne and his self-appointed squire
Rode out from Caerlyon. And young eyes watched
The flash of sunlight on a pure white shield,
And marked the glint of gold upon a helm,
And oft Ymoneth breathed a silent prayer,
For one was brother unto her, and one
Was lover, and she feared for both.

   But they,
Glad as the morning sunshine, pouring now
On fields where the tall yellow buttercups,
And thick rosettes of dandelion blooms,
And the red sorrel caught and glinted back
The colours of the sunrise, fading now

Into the blue of day,—and fair and free
In blended glow they bowed and bent amid
The billowy waves of the white hemlock clouds
Soft as the clouds above.

             And soon was reached
The valley of delight, where deep and slow
The river glided 'neath the thick-set boughs
Of trees now heavy with their summer green.
And faded all the hawthorn blooms, and gone
The golden rain of the laburnum trees,
But fruits were hung in green or rip'ning hue
On the bent boughs, and by the river side
Red-purple willow weed, and bulrush tall
Kept guard above the water-lily boats,
Moored to their roots by twisted stalks of wire ;
And honeysuckle clusters, dying down
To berries, lost themselves in wild-rose sprays
Across the grassy path.

             But as they rode,
To Ewayne's heart there came no answ'ring thrill
From what his eye beheld.   He knew the land
Was fair as any fabled for the Gods,
And yet its beauty touched no pulse of life,
Nor woke respondent joy ; and stooping down
He plucked some honeysuckle, but the flower
Was scentless as the air ;—and then he knew
That not a bird was singing overhead,

Nor was there stir of insect in the grass ;—
And turning to Sir Kynon where he rode
A little in the rear, he passed the flower
And gently said, " Methinks thou didst not tell
Thy tale aright.   Thy vale is lovely, ay,
But soul-less, empty, vain : fair to the sight,
But to the touch as cold as ice itself,
As scentless, soundless too."

           Sir Kynon paused
A moment, then rode speechless on.   But when
They reached the valley's head, he turned and gazed
Back o'er the travelled way.
           "'Tis fair indeed,
And when that morn in June I rode beneath
The snowy blossoms of the hawthorn trees,
It held for me all that my heart could wish,
And in the semblance of its brilliant glow
I rested satisfied ; the *sight* I saw,
The *scene* I could not feel, for all my sense
Was taken up with self.   I noted not
That flowers were scentless, and the birds all mute;
The vale to me was but a flow'ry path
By which to reach self-glory, and the praise
Of my poor little soul.
           " But since that day,
Two men in me have fought ; one my old self,
And one a better man, called forth by love

Of thy sweet sister, and her hopes for me.
With this I struggled, till thy words of scorn
Stung my old self to death.   Have patience now,
I pray thee, since by slow degrees at first
A life doth turn and seek to shape itself
To new and nobler forms ; and so to-day,
Though knowing that the valley lacked, indeed,
I knew not what the lack."

                    But now they turned
Through the thick beech-wood, and avoiding thus
The castle where the maidens dwelt, they soon
Approached the mound where sat the Wood-ward
        strange,
Who, at their asking, smote once more the stag,
Whereat the mound was thronged, and all the plain
Was covered as before ; and Kynon, now
Intent upon the forest creatures, felt
A wave of pity surge into his throat,
For not a cry, and no faint plaintive sound,
Broke from the living crowd ; and as he caught
The eye of fawn or timid hare, it seemed
They were beseeching him in mute appeal
For succour and release ; and turning where
Sir Ewayne stood, he saw a wondrous sight,—
For round him pressed the living waves so close
He scarce could stand ; the deer rubbed on his arm,
Red squirrels on his shoulders sat, and round

Him twined the serpents ; hares and foxes fawned
Upon his feet, and all the breathing throng
Turned to him eyes of love, more deep and strong
From pain of being mute.
    And Ewayne, he
Had lost himself, since all his soul was poured
In a rich flood of tender sympathy
To the dumb, helpless creatures at his feet ;
And Kynon, gazing on him, noted not
His face, or any feature marked distinct,
For all was merged in the great lustrous eyes,
Through which the spirit passed, a shining way,
Lit with a light from heaven.
    And when once more
The lame and one-eyed man from where he sat
Breathed over them, " Beloved, now depart,"
His voice was strangely tender, and the beasts,
As slow they wandered, feeding as they went,
Turned often to the mound where Ewayne stood,
With lingering look, and timid, anxious mien,
As wooing him to come ; while Kynon, lost
To time and space and self, was passing through
A second birth, and learning in the mute
Unconscious prayer, which, rising in regret,
Passed on to high resolve, to think and feel
With the great universe, which throbs and thrills
And suffers, ay, and ofttimes suffers most
For woes it may not speak.
  E

But once again
Sir Ewayne led the way.
"'Tis a strange land,
And under most unholy curse," quoth he;
"And my heart tells me that this same black knight,
With whom thou foughtest near the blasted tree,
Holds it in dismal thrall. Let him but die,
And all things would be well; and beast and bird
Be free to speak their love, or tell their pain,
And flowers to scent the air. And, Kynon, thou
And I this war must wage, though it be death
To thee and me": and at the ghastly thought
Of death beneath the Black Knight's sweeping lance,
Sir Kynon wavered for a moment's space,
Then, riding full abreast of Ewayne, quick
They passed into the dry and barren vale,
In midst, the single tree.
And there beside
The marble slab, on which the golden bowl
Shone yellow in the sun, the fountain played,
And Kynon thought he heard a gentle sigh
Rise with the clear blue water through the air,
And marvelled why, on that June afternoon,
When last he stood beneath the silver spray,
No sense of desolation or of pain
Had seized his heart as now; why no recoil
Had stayed his hand from waters, from whose depths
He fancied that there now gazed up at him

The living eyes of all that silent throng
Beside the grassy mound.

                " Take thou the bowl,
Sir Ewayne, thine the quest, but guard thyself
From the on-coming storm." And as the knight
Bent low above the fount, a murmuring sound
Broke through the stillness of the summer air,
And Ewayne felt himself grow fresh and strong,
And stronger as he dipped the golden bowl,
While from the blue abyss a voice breathed low,
" Drink, Ewayne, or you die ! "
                And lifting up
The shining bowl, he drank full heartily,
Then passed it on to Kynon with the words,
" Thou too must drink and live."
              And stronger still
They felt their life-blood pulsing firm and true,
Until one mighty passion surged and swayed
Their hearts within,—to meet, and fight, and slay,
That foul black knight who held the land in thrall,
Or die beneath his stroke.

              So o'er the slab
Sir Ewayne dashed the water from the bowl,
And, as before, the sky crashed overhead,
The heavens were burst asunder in blue flame,
And the bare earth rocked, trembling and afraid.

But as the tumult swelled, within their hearts
The two young knights felt firmer purpose rise,
And when the hail lashed whizzing through the air,
As on their shields they caught the icy darts,
No fear or chill could daunt the impulse fierce
That burned their hearts within.

            Then softly sweet
A murmur slowly rose; at first a sound
As of the distant sea ; and nearer still,
Of an advancing choir ; and growing loud
And louder, as the sky grew dark with birds
It swelled to great triumphant song, which thrilled
To Kynon's heart a message fraught with love,
For in the song he heard Ymoneth's voice
Sing ever the sweet words, " My knight, be strong,
I live to pray for thee ; "
            While Ewayne bowed
His head in rev'rent awe, for in the song
He heard a lady's tears flow o'er the slab,
And drop upon the bare and parchéd ground,
And grasses sprang an instant, till the storm
Burst over them, and blighted as it burst.
And now the birds, a moment free to sing,
Were chanting of the time when they must cease
And sink to silence on the dreary plain.
But Ewayne's heart went bounding forth in joy,
For now along the barren vale, a knight

On sable horse, and in black armour clad,
Rode swiftly towards the tree.

          " What mean ye, knaves,
In blighting thus my land ?   No beast is left
To wander joyful through my dewy fields ;
No leaves hang on my trees."
               But Ewayne waved
His hand towards the solitary tree,
Still greener than a pine, and where the birds
Still sang triumphantly.
          " See there thy tree ;
Through thunder and through hail no leaf has dropped,
And far across the bounds of this thy land
I see the cattle feeding in the grass,
I hear the bleat of lamb, the cry of fawn,
And all the sounds of full returning life
Awaking in thy realm."
           With that the knight
Charged full at Ewayne with so sudden shock
As well-nigh proved his fall ; but the young knight,
Avoiding it, rode out to open space
To gain an added force.

          Then waxed the fight,
As lance to lance they dashed in mad career,
And sods flew high into the beaten air,
And dust rose round them in a swirling cloud,
That oft to Kynon the two knights appeared

As figures in a dream.   And oft from where
Beside the fount he watched the furious fray,
Would he start forward in swift eager haste
To help Sir Ewayne in the deadly strife,
And then draw back, since he was but the squire,
And not unless the knight were overthrown
Could he his aid supply.
                              But watching keen,
He felt the charges, as the sable knight
With doubling fury urged his charger on,
And now great pieces of their armour flew,
Like meteors spent, through the thick dusty air,
And blood flowed fast, till Ewayne's horse, pierced
        through,
Fell dead amid the sand.   Then Kynon sprang
From his good horse, and cried, "Mount quick, my
        Lord!"
And even as he spoke, a heavy blow
Upon his shoulder blotted out the sky,
And the bare vale, and all the noise of war,
While from the spreading tree the song poured loud
And sweeter as the combat fiercer grew,
As though the singers knew the conflict o'er,
And sang of victory.

                         Then springing quick
Sir Ewayne seized the polished battle-axe
Which hung undimmed beside the gilded rein,

And swung it high in air, as the black knight
Dashed full across his path. So straight the blow
That clear it crashed through helmet and through
    skull,
And as he fell, from out the leafy tree
The birds flew o'er their foe in circling flight,
And sang their song of joy; then thrush, and lark,
And nightingale, and dove, and every bird
Sought once again its proper haunting place,
For grass was springing in the dreary vale,
And from the distant glades there came a tide
Of trailing branches, and long twisted sprays,
And soon the land was green.

        But little guessed
Sir Ewayne of this unexpected spring
Arisen in so late a summer time,
For, slipping from his horse, he lay as dead
Beside Sir Kynon on the trampled ground,
While over him the air grew softly sweet
With scent of grasses and white clover flowers,
And rabbits sported round his fallen head,
And field mice played in quiet at his feet,
And squirrels frolicked round the broken arms,
While insects woke the earth's true undertones,
And bees hummed idly by.
        At length he woke,
For o'er his brow a hand passed to and fro,

And by him knelt a lady fair and young,
With eyes of pity, in whose azure depths
He saw reflected the clear fountain's gleam,
While in the rippling sunshine of her hair
Were thread-like stems of long green water weeds,
And when she spoke, her voice came liquid sweet,
Like sound of many waters heard afar
When all the world is still :—
                    "Rise up, Sir Knight,
Thy task is now complete.   My land is freed
From that foul giant who to every man
Portrays his deadly sin.   But since that thou,
Not for thyself, but for thy kindred's sake,
Didst suffer in the fight ; and since thine heart
Is full to overflowing of the love
Of flower and tree and beast and creeping thing,
And most for human kind, 'twas thine alone
To conquer in the fray, and rid my land
Of that black curse, which year by year has spread
In blighting canker through this wretched vale,
Till scent and sound and verdure faded out,
While stronger grew the huge and dismal knight,
As every conflict left him added force
From what his foe had been.
                    " But thanks to thee
The spell is broken, and the curse is gone,
And all my land is softening into green
As fair as that once solitary tree,

Whose ever-fresh'ning branches were the sign,
That never human heart was wholly lost
To noble love, or longing after good ;
And now my birds may build in leafy grove
Or on tall forest trees, and they may sing
In early morn or in the golden eve,
And ever o'er the land their song will fall,
And not, as in the days now past and dead,
When hope renewed as some fresh conflict fell,
And o'er the promise of some opening life,
They prayed for victory."

    With that she bathed
His hands and forehead with some healing oil,
And bade him drink from out the golden bowl,
And soon, his strength renewed, he rose and sought
Sir Kynon where he lay amid the grass,
And o'er his still white face the sunshine strayed,
Flecked with the shadows of the dancing leaves,
And Ewayne thought him dead.
    But by his side
The Lady of the Fountain, stooping low,
Poured on his wounds her sweet refreshing oil,
And raised his head and murmured musingly,
" A goodly youth, too good to lose himself
In service to himself.
    " That blow he bore
And suffered for thy sake hath saved his soul

From death and deadly blight.   His sin was self,
The lower, baser self ; and that now lost
He shall attain to higher, nobler life
As all his years go on."

             And when his eyes
Were once more open to the earth and sky,
Sir Kynon knew that in another world
From that in which his former days were spent,
He should from henceforth dwell.

             So, ere the sun
Had well begun his long and slow descent,
The knights remounted, and beside the fount
They left the Lady standing 'neath the shade
Of beech and aspen, and tall linden trees,—
But when afar they turned, and halting stood,
They saw her step across the Fountain's rim,
And shining white an instant in the sun,
She sank in silence, golden bowl in hand,
To rise no more in pain.

             Then homeward straight
They rode throughout a green and flow'ry land,
Where birds now sang an evening hymn of praise,
Till in the distance rose the snowy towers
Of Caerlyon, and Kynon caught the gleam
Of sunshine falling over golden hair,
And knew Ymoneth waited at the gate.

SIR PERCIVAL AND THE CHESS-MEN.

By hill and dale,
By tower and vale,
They rode in sunny weather,
Where'er they went
On glory bent,
He and his horse together.

Beneath their feet
The earth was sweet,
For flowers bestrewed the meadows
And over head
Blooms white and red
Lit up the leafy shadows.

Oh joy of May,
When day to day
Rings out in songs of gladness,
And heart of youth
Aglow with truth
Knows little of life's sadness.

"Ope wide your gate
Ere day grow late,
Oh porter grey and olden,
The blue of night
Creeps through the light,
The West is turning golden;

"Here would we stay
Till break of day,
I and my horse together,
Till morn begun
We chase the sun
All in this spring-tide weather."

Then in they ride
Through portals wide,
Where snow-white walls are gleaming,
Where gilded towers
And ladies' bowers
Are fairer than life's dreaming;

And maidens fleet,
With voices sweet,
Around him gaily hover,
And gently lead
His dusty steed
To beds of scented clover;

And knight and squire
Bring silk attire
And shoes of 'broidered leather,
Till seated all
In castle hall
They feast and sing together;

But in and out
Amid the rout
A music soft is stealing,
And o'er the throng,
And through the song,
Light golden bells are pealing.

Oh never place
So full of grace,
So quick with wonder teeming,
Yet blended well,
That none could tell
What was, and what was seeming;

And through his heart
With sudden start
A strong fresh pulse is beating,
And life's full tide
In all its pride
Sir Percival is greeting.

The feast now done
They move anon
To bower of lady's pleasure,
A rainbow nest
Of love and rest,
And dainty beyond measure.

But sure of all
In that bright hall
Twas strange past mortal saying,
That men of gold,
With none to hold,
A game at chess were playing.

The board so bright
Was silver white,
The squares were red and yellow,
And knight and pawn
The hue of dawn
When autumn skies are mellow.

And o'er each head,
One white, one red,
A silken flag was flowing,
As in and out
They moved about,
With none to guide their going,

Until at last,
The game now past,
The tall Red King was mated,
When all his side
Rose up and cried,
" 'Tis so, for so 'twas fated ! "

Then straight and true
In order due
They stood once more completed ;
" White to begin
And Red to win
Or to be twice defeated ! "

But strange to tell,
There now befell
A new and greater wonder,
For clear and full
To Percival
The bright air burst asunder ;

And every guest
Stood there confessed,
His inner thought revealing ;
The fervent will,
Or feeble thrill,
Was plain past all concealing,

For from each dame
And knight there came,
As clear as crystal gleaming,
A shaft of thought,
Which crossed and caught
Above the chess-board streaming.

And some were keen
Like rapier clean,
And grew in ardour, fulness ;
And some like flash
Made sudden dash,
Then died away in dulness ;

And as so gay
In due array
The chess-men stood together,
With light and heat
They throbbed and beat
Like air in summer weather ;

And each man there
From off his square
Was eager to be shifted,
And half uprose
To meet his foes,
Though none there was that lifted.

King's Pawn move two,
Red Pawn move two,
White Knight comes gaily prancing,
Queen's Knight now see
On Bishop's three,
King's Bishop is advancing;

But Percival
Intent on all,
Saw how the game was guided,
That every thrill
Of thought and will
Some motive power provided.

And noting well
What chance befell,
He saw past all denying,
That fiercest beam
Of all the stream
Of light upon them lying,

Fell on the White
From lady bright,
The Lady of the Bower,
Whose glances dread
To foil the Red,
And aid the White had power.

F

So in the game
The clever dame
Her own strong will was playing,
And each gold man,
Of her deep plan
Some dictate was obeying.

Then keen and strong
There passed along
A counter stream of action,
And Red men all,
Both great and small,
Thrilled to a new attraction ;

And Bishop now
Refused to bow
Before the Lady's order,
But to the game
The King's Knight came
And threw it in disorder.

Then sharp and quick
Like hailstones thick
The pieces moved like magic,
And Red and White
Rushed to the fight
With fury that was tragic,—

The lady bent
With full intent
To see the Red King mated,
Found with dismay
Her power decay
And saw the White King fated.

As in the past
She proudly cast
Her spell on one and other,—
Red men would turn
Her way to learn,
Then quickly take another ;

And even White
Refused outright
To move to all her willing,
And now and then
Her golden men
Were some new law fulfilling.

And every guest
Felt in his breast
A pulse of passion beating,
Each took a side,
And each one tried,
In the wild game competing.

But swift and sure,
Each step secure,
The White King stood confounded,
By Red Queen here,
And Bishop there,
And castle all surrounded.

And every guest
As seemed him best
Cried out in wrath or pleasure ;
But like a fire
The Lady's ire
Was kindled beyond measure.

And looking full
At Percival,—
" Thine is the fault," she shouted ;
" 'Tis by thine aid
My plans are laid
And all my men are routed !

" And not alone
For glory won
Have golden men been playing,
But for thy soul,
Thy life's control,
Thy purpose, and thy praying ;

" With full intent
I surely meant
To have thy will in guiding,
My name is Fate,
And here I wait
For souls in me confiding ;

"And every guest
Means some behest,
Some current good or evil,
Some impulse rife
About the life,
Some angel, or some devil.

" Yet now and then
'Mong mortal men
Comes one, on self reliant,
Who scorns to wait
The doom of Fate,
Who turns on us defiant ;

" Then 'tis we know
That we must bow,
That man has passed our portal,
And good and ill
Not Fate fulfil,
But life that is immortal ;

" And far and wide,
Whate'er betide,
O'er circumstance exultant,
He lays his will
On good and ill,
And ends at last, triumphant."

Then faded out
The noise and rout,
And gentle slumber stealing,
Brought rest and calm
And healing balm
And dreams new truth revealing,

Till morn begun,
To chase the sun,
Sir Percival rode lightly
From castle gate,
Where ladies wait
'Mid rose trees blooming brightly,

For Spring had gone,
And now anon
Through hot and Summer weather,
Sir Percival
Rode down the dale,
He and his horse together.

THE RESURRECTION BODY.

THIS body, we know it from head to foot,
From heel to crown ;
And sometimes we love it,
When days are fair ;
And sometimes we hate it,
And sigh to bear
The stain on the soul
Of a lost control,
And account it a clog, and a load of care
To keep us down.

But what if this body were but a sheath
For quickened bud ?
And suppose that the life,
Thus hid from sight,
And preserved by it
From blast and blight,
Be just what we all
By the one name call
Of spirit, or soul ? but though named aright
Not understood ;

And suppose that the bud by an innate force
　　Should slow unfold?
　　And compelled by a power
　　　We term divine,
　　And cultured by weather
　　　Of shade and shine,
　　Should assume the form
　　Which the sun and storm
Of what we call life in this world, combine
　　To shape and mould?

Till at length the sheath can no more retain
　　The bursting bud,
　　But withered and useless
　　　It drop away,
　　One body made perfect
　　　As one decay;
　　Will it then appear
　　That while even here,
We fashioned a body for some great day,
　　Then understood?

That body! what form it shall henceforth take
　　Is past our ken;
　　But sometimes we can feel
　　　Its pulses beat,
　　And we use even now
　　　Its hands and feet;

The light of its eyes
On a smile oft lies ;
But what it shall be when all is complete,
Is kept till then.

————

AND FURTHER STILL.

That body ! we cannot as yet declare
Its next abode,
And sometimes we fancy
That even here,
In this old world planet,
We re-appear ;
Or does it arise
To new earth and skies ?
What matter the place, if it be more near,
More close to God ?

And what of the life ? In the world that now
We seem to know,
The truest of union
We hope to find,
Consists in the mingling
Of mind with mind,

Where love, in one whole,
Knits a soul with soul,
Yet neither consciousness lose, though combined
In even flow;

Then suppose that within some further sphere
Two souls there be,
And suppose they have reached
The self-same place,
In thinking, and feeling,
In love, and grace,
And they there unite
And commingle quite,
Would either lose, in this presupposed case,
Its identity?

Then might it not be that in worlds beyond,
Remoter still,
The process repeated
Through countless years,
More perfect becoming
In purer spheres,
All the æons past,
It shall be at last,
Not God and another, but One appears
The One great Will?

THE FIRST DAY IN A WOOD.

WE were Johnnie, and Tom, and Katie,
    Sometimes, but not always, good ;
Long ago, on a fresh spring morning,
    We entered a spring-tide wood ;
The sun sparkled down in the shadows,
    In wonderful twists and twirls,
As the leaves danced high in the sunshine,
    As lightly as Katie's curls ;
We were all quite fresh from the city,
    Knew little of birds and trees,—
We had heard there were eggs and wild-flowers,
    And our hearts were bent on these ;—
But just on the skirts of the wild wood
    We paused, for there came a hush
Right out of the heart of the shadows,
    And breathed from each tree and bush :
'Twas a magic touch to the heart strings,
    And the wood became a church,
And we gazed down the aisles in wonder,
    Of tremulous ash and birch ;
The angels were singing above us,

Hid from our sight in the trees,—
The organ played softly and sweetly,
   Though 'twas but the spring-tide breeze ;
Then gently we stepped through the green-wood
   And knelt where the primrose grew,
And we trod with delicate rapture
   The glades of hyacinth blue ;
We caught the last gleam of the wind-flower
   And of the celandine star,
And the keen strong scent of the pink-thorn
   Fell o'er us from tree-tops far ;
And Katie bent over the fern-fronds
   To watch their tight curls unfold,
And the sunny gleam of her ringlets
   Was lost in the cowslip gold ;—
And now she is gone from the glory
   That woke in our hearts that day,
To some other wonder of beauty
   Which may not be far away ;
And Johnnie and Tom are no longer
   The children who stood that morn
In the golden gleam of the green-wood
   The day that their souls were born,—
But in fancy, amid life's failures,
   They stand as that day they stood,
And long for the freshness of wonder
   Of that first day in a wood.

SELF AND NOT-SELF.

My Self, does it stand for one, alone,
    Is it only I?
And how far beyond my identity
    Does the not-self lie?
And what is the value, and what the force
    Of the My, and Me?
And where in the conflict with might and right
    Can the true self be?

For it oft-times seems that the law of self
    Is a law of blood,
That beneath its ruthless and tyrant reign
    Can arise no good
Except to the strong; that the few may stand
    Where the many fall,
And only the fit shall survive in time
    The struggle of all.

But surely not so was the round earth planned,
    And not such the rule,
For the self to grow to its purport true
    In the human school,—

Since in man and state has the progress come,
    Where his aims have been
In the sweeter life, and ultimate good,
    Of the not-self seen ;

So the noblest mind is the substance caught
    From the not-self vast,
And then back in thought, or in burning word
    On the current cast ;
And the moral force of a cultured soul
    Is the outward flow
Of the life received, and that now must beat
    In some pulse more slow.

And what we call love, is the reaching forth,
    Is the soul intent,
Is the thought and life, is indeed the self
    On the not-self spent ;
And each love absorbed, new forces unfold
    As new needs arise,
Till what had its birth in mere selfishness,
    Ends in sacrifice.

For the self has reached to the secret source
    Of the love divine,
And has learnt to blend in a God-like way
    What was Mine, and Thine ;

And so, as the self is transformed to soul,
Can be understood,
That the law which rules in the universe
Is a law of Good.

THE DREAMERS.

ASLEEP! Ah no; the dream-land true
   Is not where sudden fancies creep
From the dim vistas of the night
   Down the long corridors of sleep;—

But rather, 'tis a land aflame,
   And lit by suns whose burning rays
Will fall reflected on the stream
   Of common life in future days;

And in whose blue and rugged steeps,
   Which tower within the light sublime,
There rise the everlasting rills
   Of common thought for years of time.

And they who dream, think not they lie
   In languid glades of scented ease,
Or under sunny skies recline
   Lulled into rest by sapphire seas;

Not so ; each dreamer as he wakes
　Alone, upon that mystic shore,
Is lured along its winding way
　By shad'wy form which goes before,

And he must follow when the path
　Is through fair meadows deep in grass ;
Nor faint when over arid sand
　Or flinty rock his feet must pass ;

For what is shadow in that land,
　And what in vision has its birth,
Transmuted through long years of thought
　Is substance for the common earth ;

And caught along the wings of dream
　That which has once Ideal been,
Is floated on from age to age
　And is in time the Real seen.

So one may dream of ladder set,
　And angel forms with golden hair
Descending from ethereal heights
　To mount again the shining stair,

And man will learn that wastes untrod,
　That through the old and in the new
No spot but has its climbing way
　To link it with the arch of blue.

And on the mount, behind the cloud,
  One forty days may dream with God,
Then walk again, with shining face,
  The shrouded path so lately trod.

And man shall learn the guilt of sin,
  And kneel in silence and in awe,
Beneath the clouds from which there burst
  The lightnings of eternal law.

And some have dreamed 'mid Judah's hills,
  Or in Samaria's golden halls,
Or where upon Euphrates' strand
  The hot salt tear of exile falls,

Of cities white beneath the sun,
  No more defiled by idol fame,
Whose towers and pinnacles arise
  From temples true to Jahveh's name.

They died, but not the dream, for lo,
  In Attic land it wakes again,
And steals in silence down the aisles
  And sunny glades of branching plane ;

And with no sound of him who builds,
  A state arises strong and new,
Where Justice, Temperance, Chastity,
  And Knowledge are alone the true ;

Where service shall be sought, not shunned,
   And right be universal rule,
And he who gathers gold in store
   Shall be by most accounted fool.

Thus common customs, civic rights,
   Are but a reflex and a gleam,
And men have formed their purest laws
   From out the fabric of a dream.

And from Utopias new and old,
   And from Arcadian fields afar,
Those visions of perfection come
   Which put to shame the things that are.

And one has vision vast and deep,
   Of all the circling steeps that rise
From lurid depths of seething hell
   To whitest light of Paradise ;

And one on Malvern's sunny slope
   Dreams of the seriousness of life,
While o'er the field all full of folk
   There floats the hum of human strife ;

Or on a dewy morn reclined
   Within a green and verdant bower,
One dreams the beauty of the leaf
   Is perfect as the rarest flower ;

Or through a dungeon damp and dark
Rays of supernal glory stream,
For there the golden streets and gates
Of the Celestial City gleam ;

And earth and heaven draw near apace,
Nor small nor great there now appears,
And man has learnt that life and time
Know not the limit-span of years.

And some have dreamed, and forces new
From waiting nature have been caught,
And pole draws nearer unto pole
As man moves swift on wings of thought ;

And deep beneath the roar of loom,
And through the whirr of countless wheels,
And from the avenues of art,
The vision of the dreamer steals ;

And as fulfilled each great design,
And things once new grow dim or die,
Still further heights of sunrise gold
Shall dawn upon the dreamer's eye ;

Till slowly grows the perfect sphere,
And years and life shall never fail
Some mind to mould a nobler state,
Some soul to seek a holier Graal.

A BIRTHDAY.

Your birthday, and I sit and ponder here
    Beneath the summer sky ;
I gaze above at the broad arch of blue,
And try with aching eyes to pierce it through,
That I might see you for a moment, Dear,
    Within your home on high.

Long years ago, they came to me one night
    And told me you were dead.
They took you from the waters cold and deep,
The waters that had lulled you into sleep,
They laid you with your young face pale and white
    Upon your quiet bed.

I saw you lie, the lips that I had kissed,
    So blue, and cold, and chill ;
Your eyes were closed, and there across your breast
The busy loving hands were crossed, at rest ;
But more than all your loving smile I missed,
    And life was dark and still.

They took you up with gentle rev'rent care,
      And bore you to your home ;
Within the warm sweet earth they laid you, Dear,
And bitter tears were shed above your bier,
Then turned with broken hearts and left you there
      Deep in your quiet tomb.

But *you* were not within that lowly cell
      Beneath the sunny wold ;
It was not *you* I saw so still and white,
It was not *you* I kissed that summer night,
Had it been *you* could I have said farewell,
      And left you lone and cold ?

It was not *you* I gazed at with hot eyes
      That ached for lack of tears ;
You would have turned to smile into my face,
And clasp me to you in a close embrace ;
You loved to please me with some glad surprise,
      And calm my foolish fears.

Where did you go, my Love, that summer night,
      The night you left me here ?
What pathway did your deathless spirit take,
While I, with stony heart that would not break,
Gazed after you into the starry height,
      And missed, yet felt you near ?

Into what land did your freed spirit glide,
      Where are you now, my Love?
And in the land where you are gone to dwell,
Do you remember her you loved so well,
Or is your soul quite full and satisfied
      There in your home above?

And do you think sometimes of earthly things,
      The life that used to be?
Do you remember our sweet summer walks,
And do you now recall our evening talks,
Or aught that happened ere your soul took wing
      And went so far from me?

What are you learning there in that far land,
      The land you now call home?
And do you treasure up the knowledge deep,
And think of me sometimes, and try to keep
A vacant place beside you, as you stand
      And watch for me to come?

I cannot come to you, perhaps, for years,
      But, Love, from time to time,
I feel you near me in my lonely sleep,
I feel the shadow of your love so deep,
I seem to draw you by my very tears
      From your far distant clime.

Your birthday, Dear! do you remember it,
  As I do here below?
And do you look from out the sunny skies,
And smile with deeper love in your pure eyes,
To see how here alone on earth I sit
  And wait, yet long to go?

For when the wayside flowers are blooming fair,
  And summer skies are blue,
I hear you calling me in accents sweet,
I feel you drawing me above, to meet
You once again, your inmost life to share,
  I fain would come to you.

Your birthday, Dear! you keep it up above,
  I keep it here to-day;
And yet united in the solemn hush
Of silence, do our souls together rush,
And mingle in a never-dying love,
  Which knoweth no decay.

THE WAYSIDE.

THOUGH garden grounds are rich and fair
   Yet sweeter are the by-ways,
And good it is to wander far
   From parks and well-kept highways;
To leave behind neat close-trimmed lawns,
   And beds in glowing ray dyed,
To revel in the tangled growth
   Of some scarce trodden wayside.

Look, here's a lane, a narrow lane,
   Not more than half a mile long,
But oh, the undertone of sound
   That mingles with the birds' song;
The hum of bee, the buzz of fly,
   The creak of unseen corn-crake,
And in the grass the constant stir
   Which grasshoppers and ants make.

And here's a bank, crowned on the top
   With blackberry and roses,
And underneath a tangled growth,
   A matted wealth of posies,

St. John's-wort creeping everywhere,
   And star-wort dotted over,
And lower down, beside the road,
   A head or two of clover;

And there some blue forget-me-not,
   And up above, a foxglove,
Then underneath, some daisy roots,
   And sprigs of scented wood-ruff;
And tall, deep, yellow buttercups
   Mixed up with airy hemlock,
And here a tuft of lady fern
   Which hides a modest shamrock.

And now a bit of broken wall,
   With lichen spread upon it,
With polypods, and tufts of grass,
   And mosses growing on it;
And next, a bit of softest turf,
   So green and sweetly fallow,
And then another tangled bank,
   And further on some mallow.

And here a pale campanula
   In stately isolation,
And then an ivy-girdled hedge
   That borders a plantation;

Above our heads tall chestnut trees,
    While at our feet are springing
Some tender shoots of pale green oak
    With bind-weed round them clinging.

And here's a reedy weedy ditch
    With meadow-sweet and rushes,
And crowfoot creeping round the roots
    Of dark-leaved alder bushes ;
Veronica and watercress,
    An undergrowth of mosses,
And on the edge huge water-docks,
    With flowers in purple bosses ;

Tall willow-weeds and bergamot
    With campion among them,
And blue and yellow water-flags,
    Which love the streams and throng them ;
And then a bank of strawberry,
    With white stars dotted over,
And next some more forget-me-not,
    And larger, redder clover.

So on and on adown the lane
    We wander, scarcely thinking,
While all the time the thirsty soul
    Is deep of beauty drinking ;—

Till out again into the dust
  And bareness of the highway,
We sigh, as we remember all
  The sweetness of the by-way.

I HEARD A VOICE.

I HEARD a voice
Which said to me "Cry!"
And I answered quick,—
"What, what shall I cry?
Shall I take my stand
In the crowded street,
Shall I stop the rush
Of the eager feet,
And above the throb
Of the loom and wheel,
Shall I cry aloud
With a thunder-peal,—
"Haste, haste ye on
In the race for wealth,
Young men in the glow
Of youth and health,
Get all the good
That this world can give,
To-morrow we die,
To-day we live!
Life, life to you

Should be fair and bright,
So with eager heart
And with footstep light,
Take all the pleasure
That youth can buy,
Eat ! drink ! grow rich,
To-morrow you die.

" And you who are old
And bowed with care,
Who think that life
Has been hardly fair ;
Who have fought and failed
And lost all hope,
Till now worn out
You stagger and grope ;
What matters a few
Short years, and then,
Poor, suffering, wretched,
Ill-starred men,
You shall be as good
As a lord of state,
For to rich and poor
There comes one fate ;
Lo, here I stand
And ye hear me cry,
' To-day we mourn,
To-morrow we die !' "

I heard a voice
Which said to me " Cry !"
And I answered quick,
" What, what shall I cry ?
Shall I stand by kings
In their pomp and show,
And cry in their ears
In tone of woe ;—
Haste, haste ye fools,
In the race for power,
Ye kings with the wide-
Spread lands for dower ;
Annex, destroy,
Go to war, kill, kill,
Though the nations groan
Take ye your fill ;
A king must live
Though the people die,
What matter a vulgar
Tear or sigh ?
Spread out your rod
O'er a wide domain,
And add new lands
To your lustrous reign,
Toil on, till cold
And alone you lie,
To-day you rule,
To-morrow you die.

" And you who strive
'Mid the toil and heat,
The smoke and grime
Of the miry street,
To keep your souls
From the blast and blight,
Your truth unspoiled,
And your garments white,—
Who stretch strong hands
To the faint and weak,
And through the desert
The lost ones seek ;—
Though ye sometimes fall
And oft-times fail,
And life runs on
Like an ill-told tale,
Toil on, toil on,
As the moments fly,
To-morrow you live
Though to-day you die."

THE BROOK SONG.

Tinkle, bubble, and gush,
  Tumble and toss along,
Singing as over the stones I rush,
  Oh such a merry song;
Gurgle, gabble, and splash,
  Ripple and romp all day,
Singing as onward I leap and dash
  A song so blithe and gay.

Tinkle, tinkle,
The bluebells ring
As they dance in the sunshine fair,
Warble, warble,
The birdies sing
As they wheel in the summer air;
Rustle, rustle,
The reeds reply
As they bend in the scented breeze;
While buzz, and buzz,
From flow'rets by,
Comes the hum of contented bees.

Bending her graceful head,
    The meadow-sweet sings to me,
And the roses blush to a rosy red
    Up there on the leafy tree ;
Mosses with silent feet
    Creep ever my banks along,
And far o'erhead the cloudlets meet,
    And join in the happy song.

Dazzle, the sun shines high,
    Glitter, the moon smiles cold,
Twinkle the stars in the far off sky,
    Shimmering points of gold ;
While tinkle, bubble, and gush,
    Tumble and toss along,
Away to the sea I gaily rush,
    Singing my merry song.

THE ROSE OF BETHLEHEM.

(A LEGEND OF GERMANY.)

He rides swift through a lonely land,
   Sir Karl the Eagle-eye,—
And 'neath his courser's lightning tread
   The long miles hasten by.

His steed, it is of glossy brown,
   And fleet as passing wind,
Search north and south, search east and west,
   Its peer you will not find.

And never knight more firmly sat,
   And never knight more true,
As aye before his straining sight
   A picture rose anew,—

A maiden fresh as morning light
   Sits in her stately halls,
While at her feet, with head bent low,
   A humble suitor falls.

An anxious look is on her face,
　A tear is in her eye,
And from her red and parted lips
　There comes a gentle sigh ;—

" I know you noble, brave, and true,
　My heart is sore distressed ;
I would my life had been quite free,
　That none had love professed ;

" I would that in the convent shade
　My soul had found a home,
Where no fond dream of earthly joy,
　Or human love had come ;

" Where I in the long coming years
　Might be the bride of Heaven ;—
But now I hear another voice,
　Another call is given.

" But ere I yield thee all my love,
　Ere I be wholly thine,
Go seek for me a sacred gift,
　A treasure all divine ;

" A rose, plucked from a budding tree,
　That grew beside the shed,
Where our dear Lord first lay at rest
　Upon His manger-bed.

" It was not yet the time of flowers,
　　But laid upon his breast,
　The bud unfolded full and fair,
　　In that sweet presence blest ;

" And the young mother, smiling, took
　　The flow'ret for her own,
　And hid it 'mid her precious things,
　　In token of her son ;

" And as the day dawns year by year,
　　That saw our Saviour's birth,
　That saw the blessed Prince of Peace
　　Descend to bless our earth,

" That flow'ret feels the touch of life,
　　Its withered leaves unclose,
　And year by year it blooms again,
　　A blushing Christmas Rose ;

" Now guarded in a crystal vase,
　　Within a convent grim,
　In the old town of Bethlehem,
　　That rose lies brown and dim ;

" But when it next doth flush to life,
　　As sound the bells of Yule,
　I would behold the glorious sight,
　　Holy and wonderful.

"Go ride thou then on thy good steed,
    Haste thee, oh haste away,
And bring to me the mystic flower
    For which my heart doth pray;

"And I will give to thee my hand,
    My heart, my soul, my life;
Go! when I see the flower bloom forth,
    Then claim me for thy wife."

He rides alone at noon's high glare,
    And in the evening light,
Eastward through sun, and shower, and shade,
    Eastward by day and night.

He rides where forest arches high
    Grow yellow, brown, and red,
As autumn tints the mighty trees,
    And leaves sink 'neath his tread.

So swift he speeds, for time is short,
    While through the ghostly nights
Strange shapes are seen, and down the paths
    Gleam pale and spectral lights.

But on and on he holds his way,
    Stops but for needed rest,
And strives, by headlong speed, to still
    The fever of his breast.

And when the simple wayside folk
   Beg him to rest and pray,
He faster pricks his noble steed,
   And onward keeps his way.

What boots it that before him lie
   Long miles of toilsome road,
Dark woods, steep hills, wide open tracks,
   And water-courses broad ;

His way is over them, and on
   That eastern town to win,
Then with his treasure safely grasped
   His western course begin.

Yet wild and wan his face became,
   His steed grew gaunt and spare,
Until up Bethlehem's street at length
   They ride, a spectral pair.

Ah, monkish hearts are ill to move,
   They scoff at love's strong plea,
Yet harder far than granite rock
   The human heart would be,

That, gazing on that wasted form,
   That wild and sunken eye,
Could turn away unmoved, or, cold,
   The earnest prayer deny.

And love may pierce through convent walls,
   However grim they seem,
And wake to new and living birth
   Some long forgotten dream ;

So with the precious crystal vase
   Pressed close unto his breast,
Sir Karl rode from the ancient town,
   And turned him to the west.

And ever as he rode along,
   The days grew short and chill,
And in the afternoon, the sun
   Set red behind the hill ;

And bare and dark the branches waved,
   Their leaves all strewed around,
While 'mid the naked boughs, the wind
   Moaned with a fitful sound ;

And swiftly as he rode along,
   The children fled in fear,
And peasants crossed themselves in dread,
   To see a ghost so near.

December skies were growing dark,
   And soon the Yule-tide bell
O'er all the waiting, watching earth
   Its tale of peace would tell ;

And he had far, ay, far to ride,
  So many miles to go,
When there came softly floating by
  A flake of whitest snow ;

So soft it fell, 'twas like a plume
  Dropped from an angel's wing,
And yet Sir Karl urged on his horse
  And made him faster spring ;

But not so swift that lightning steed
  As came those flakes so white,
They filled the air, they fell and fell
  All through the lonely night ;

And far around on field and wood
  There sank a silence dread,
While through a weird and spectral world
  The horse and rider fled,

From night to morn, and then was seen
  No path, no guiding track ;
Nothing to break the spotless white
  But their own shadows black.

Yet still Sir Karl bore bravely on,
  His task would soon be o'er ;—
Through brake and wood, up-hill and glen,
  By plain, and moss, and moor.

And oft, to cheer his drooping heart,
  He saw in fancy bright,
His lady gazing wistful forth
  Across the fields of white.

The light of love is in her eyes,
  But pale her face with fear,
Lest she have asked a boon too hard
  From one she holds so dear.

And then he urges on his steed
  Through the deep drifts of snow,
While from the sky, the sombre clouds
  Hang thick, and black, and low.

But slowly, slowly do they wend
  Across the world so still,
And now the last, the trysting day,
  Is dawning o'er the hill,

And many miles are still to ride
  And it is far to go ;—
Sir Karl's good horse sinks headlong down,
  Dead, 'mid the drifts of snow.

No time to weep, no time to sigh,
  To mourn his charger's fate,
He must away with wingéd feet,
  On, ere it be too late.

And swift he fled that dreary day,
   Until, as evening fell,
He heard far off across the snow
   The pealing of a bell.

The holy bell of Yule-tide swung
   And called on men to pray, —
To him, the soft and distant chime
   But onward urged his way.

With weary feet and stiffened limb,
   A figure gaunt and dread,
Most like a wan and ghastly corpse
   New risen from the dead.

Yet still the bells ring softly sweet,
   And lure him gently on,
They stir anew his frozen blood,
   For hope is in the tone.

The moon is rising through the clouds,
   Midnight is dawning clear,
When to a church's open door
   Sir Karl at length drew near.

He knows that there his lady sweet
   Will come at midnight deep,
Within the chancel's sacred shade
   A holy watch to keep,

And he would meet her there to-night,
  And, kneeling at her feet,
Yield up his precious gift, and know
  His task of love complete.

He reached the porch, but, faint and spent,
  Across the path he fell,
While high above, the Christmas chime
  Rang out a soft death knell :—

And nearer came a glancing light
  Across the fallen snow,
And nearer came dark shrouded forms,
  And voices chanting low,

As to the sacred lone retreat
  The noble lady came,
With her young maidens, there to bless
  The holy Mother's name,—

To kneel before the Virgin shrine,
  With heart of anxious love,
While o'er the still and silent earth
  The bells ring sweet above.

But see ! Across the snow-clad path,
  What still and dark form lies ?
A pang of dread strikes to her heart,
  And tears crowd to her eyes,—

For well she knows that longed-for face,
    Although so pale and wan,
And well she knows that noble form,
    Though wasted to the bone ;

But lo ! upon his hollow breast
    Was seen a wondrous sight,
A Rose, all blooming fresh and fair
    In the cold wintry night ;

It shone with lustre bright and clear,
    Too pure for flower of earth,
While overhead the bells rang out
    The blessed Saviour's birth,—

And with a cry that rang afar
    Across the spotless snows,
The lady sank beside her lord,
    Beside the blushing Rose,

She clasped his neck, she kissed his cheek,
    Then overhead, the bell
Rang out for lord and lady fair,
    A double, loud death-knell.

And on the spot in after years,
    A tree grew tall and green ;
The like in all the country round
    Was never known, I ween ;

For when the blesséd Yule-tide bell
  Rings out across the snows,
A flower blooms forth in beauty rare,
  A blushing Christmas Rose.

POETS AND CRITICS.

Poets write as nature bids them,
　　Sing forsooth because they must,
Prompted by the inspiration
　　Of a great and holy trust ;—

Yet they never reach the passion
　　That is stirring heart and brain ;
Cannot show the depth and longing
　　In their pleasure or their pain ;

So they crave some richer medium
　　Than the cold word-forming pen,
Pray for some more faithful outlet
　　To convey their thoughts to men.

Critics write as fancy takes them,
　　Vent the feelings of an hour,
Prompted by the contradiction
　　Of their wish, yet want of power.

So they oft-times blame the poet
    For some thought not finely said,
And forget his words are heart-beats,
    Theirs, the wisdom of the head.

Or they show, past all denying,
    That his thought and creed are wrong,
Sure that they, more than the singer,
    Know the import of the song.

While the poet, too, bemoaning
    Want of power in human speech,
Burdened with his deep heart-longings,
    Sighing, some great truth to teach,—

Joins himself unto the critics,
    Owns the truth of what they say,
Feels his weakness, well-nigh failure,—
    But of them would humbly pray :

Have they ever tried to prison
    Wingéd thought that wakes, then flies,
Tried to fathom all the passion
    In the human heart that lies?

Then with soul aflame and eager
    Tried to set it forth in verse,
Tried with words the thought to marry
    Or the glowing mood rehearse ?

Have they ever thrilled and trembled
  At the sum of human wrong?
Ever gauged the fierce wild conflict
  Waged between the right and wrong?

Are their minds so sympathetic
  That they act in others' deeds?
Are their natures quick, responsive
  To the touch of others' needs?

And when strung to high soul-transport,
  Have they ever tried to pen,
All their love, and all their longing,
  All their sympathy with men?

Have they ever tried to picture
  All that in a landscape fair
Calls to the imagination,
  All the beauties hidden there?

Tried to tell in words full worthy
  The strange mystic power that lies
In the crimson far-off glory
  Of the western sunset skies?

Tried to speak in thundrous numbers
  Of the ocean's deaf'ning roar,
Or to lisp the gentle lappings
  Of the tide upon the shore?

I

Tried to sing the quiet teachings
　　Of the calm and silent night,
And the ceaseless inspiration
　　Born on earth in morning light?

Oh the poet, bound and fettered
　　To a ministry of words,
Sorrows oft that his expression
　　With his feeling ill accords.

He would speak with such a passion,
　　Sing with such o'erwhelming might,
That the world in wonder listening
　　Would be shamed into the right.

He would spread soft soothing numbers
　　O'er the weary, worn with care;
Help the sorrow-laden toilers
　　All their load of life to bear.

Ask the artist if he ever
　　Gained the perfectness he sought,
If the finished canvas ever
　　Quite conveyed his inmost thought?

Can the purest strains of music
　　More than shadow forth, at best,
The sublime and high ideal
　　In the great composer's breast?

Blended chord and rampant chorus,
   Liquid sweet harmonic swell,
Feebly show the thought impassioned
   Which he tries, yet fails to tell.

And the sculptor prays from heaven
   Gift of life for perfect form,
That his glowing thought embodied
   May be seen, full, true, and warm.

Ay, the human heart has longings
   Deeper, stronger, richer far
Than the best of painted pictures,
   Music, song, or poems are.

So the poet sinks faint-hearted,
   Knows his strongest efforts weak,
Tries again, and strives on ever,
   Through his failures growing meek,—

Till at last he sighs in singing :
   I shall not have toiled in vain,
If one human life be brightened,
   If one heart feel less of pain ;

If one noble aspiration
   Has been stirred by word of mine ;
Speech, though feeble, poor, and faulty,
   May convey a spark divine.

Poets too, becoming critics,
  Might for once the tables turn,
How have men used their endeavours,
  Thoughts that teach and words that burn?

Have they not some cause for grieving
  When they hear their choicest gem
Parodied by careless reader,
  Dead alike to it, and them?

O'er the page sublime of Milton
  Listen to the school-boy's sigh,
Searching out the nouns objective,
  And the verbs they're governed by.

Shakspeare's verse reduced to parsing,
  Scanned and analysed by some
Who fulfil his words of foresight,
  "To vile uses do we come."

And the teacher, shrewd and knowing,
  Smiles to find the poet wrong;
"Count the accents on your finger
  And you'll find the line too long."

So the poet's deep heart-searchings,
  Thoughts of which his soul was full,
Serve for truant's imposition,
  Help the routine of the school.

But he knows the few will bless him,
   Thank him for the word of hope,
Thank him for a ray to lighten
   The dark path in which they grope ;

Thank him for the glimpses opened
   Into far sublimer spheres,
For the unattained ideals
   Looming through the mist of years.

Thank him for the faint dim prelude
   Of the song which he might sing
In a land by spirits haunted,
   Where no earth could clog or cling,—

He a spirit unto spirits
   Pouring out his inmost soul ;
They in sympathetic union
   Making one harmonious whole.

VIOLIN SOLO.

LEGENDE IN G MINOR.

IT spoke ;—
The yielding air at the magic touch
Caught up the tone of the long-drawn note,
Then rose and fell as a joyous flood
From its soul in ecstasy there broke.
Ay, strong is youth, and it hopes for much,
And visions fair in the future float,
And the opening world is wide and free,
And to swift young feet the years come slow ;
The heart is full as the clear sweet strain
That softer grew to swell out again,
Till it throbbed and thrilled, a wondrous glow
Of high born hope for the life untrod ;
An eager rush of the quivering strings,
Like a young heart seeking sublimer things.

And yet through all, through the witching tone,
Through the flood of song that rose and fell,

One voice was heard, and but one alone.
The notes were pure, and sweet, and high,
But the cadence rang so clear to tell,
That the deeper pulses of the soul
Were yet untouched in their infant sleep ;
That yet untouched was the mystic deep
Of its own wild restless passion's sweep ;—
The fiery fight, and the clouds that roll,
And the winds that come the heart to try,
Were yet unknown, as the morning light
Dreams not of the storms that come ere night.
So the notes rolled on, they grew and grew,
Till the verge of Life at last they reach ;—
But listen !   What is it deep and new
That steals along in a fuller strain ?
Scarce heard at first, but an undertone,
A tender touch as of coming pain,—
Then a deeper note, a richer flow,
And the voice has ceased to sing alone ;—
And mingling, blending, joyous and strong,
The flood grows swifter and sweeps along
With the tender grace of youth and love,
And the chords more full and perfect grow,
And open out as two hearts awake,
Approach, retreat,—then in blended sweep
In full duet doth the music break,
Until all the pulsing air around
Can scarce contain the deep flood of sound.

Then a sudden pause; the air grows still
And sobs itself into quiet rest;
Till again there breaks in a monotone
The sound of a voice that sings alone.
Alone, but not as the first glad note
That spoke of a soul not yet awake,
A note that told how a joyous chord
Into fuller life should reach and break;
But alone, with something lost for aye,
With a light gone out ere evening come;
An empty void which no voice can fill,
A throbbing wound which no hand can still:
The chords are rent, all the strings are mute
Save one that in solitude rings low,
And with broken accents strives to show
How dark and deep is the lone heart's woe.

But there stealing comes, like the gentle wind
That stirs in the drooping trees at even,
A hope, that seems in its new calm swell
To drop from the over-arching heaven:
So faint at first as to almost seem
But the echo of some far-off dream;
We scarce can tell if the strain is caught
From some fond loved mem'ry of the past;
Or down from celestial harpers cast;
Till there thrills again from the saddened strings
A chaste pure song of regret and hope,

That floats aloft to the love-lit land,
The land where the broken chords at last
Shall meet and flow in a perfect strain,
That shall know no discord nor sad refrain.

SONG OF THE SEASONS.

When trees are greening overhead,
    And daffodils are yellow,
When daisies bend beneath our tread,
    And primroses are mellow ;
When streams are leaping fresh and bright
    New life and verdure bringing,
And birds from early morn to night
    Their songs of love are singing ;—
Oh life is then a joyous thing,
    Our hearts beat strong and lightly,
For all around in robes of Spring,
    Fair Earth, she smileth brightly.

When roses bloom upon the bough,
    And foxgloves deck the hedges ;
When lazily the waters flow
    Among the reeds and sedges ;
When skies are glowing blue and high,
    And fields with grass are waving,
While cattle in the pond hard by
    Their burning feet are laving ;—
'Tis then we feel our pulses beat
    With manhood's strong endeavour.

The Summer of our life we greet,
    And Spring is gone for ever.

When apples drop from laden trees,
    And golden sheaves are binding ;
When heather scents are in the air,
    And hunter's horn is winding ;
When barns are filled with ample store
    Of Nature's kind providing,
And sky and earth are crimsoned o'er,
    In golden light abiding ;—
Oh then we feel glad Autumn's glow,
    The fruit of life's stern pressure ;—
The Summer flower aside we throw,
    The Autumn fruit we treasure.

When winds are roaring high and shrill,
    And stainless snows are falling,
When frost has locked the waters chill
    Within its grasp enthralling ;
When holly berries bright and red,
    From dark green bowers are peeping,
While naked branches toss o'erhead,
    And bud and bird are sleeping ;—
We too would sink to Winter's sleep,
    Our sun is near the setting,
In life we sow, and toil, and reap,
    Then comes the long forgetting.

THE WONDERFUL LAND.

A Wonderful Land my soul hath seen ;
   The portals opened wide,
I entered amid the glory, where
   The great red sun had died ;
Through the crimson gates of the gleaming west
   Drawn in by an unseen hand,
Led on by the music of angel songs,
   Lured into the Wonderful Land ;
All bathed in the warmth of the sunset sky
   Thrilled through with the golden light ;
Beyond the clouds and beyond the sun,
   Beyond the reach of night.

My heart had longed for that lovely land,
   And in the radiant glow
My spirit had tried full oft to sink,
   My soul had wished to go ;
And night by night as the glory grew
   And the west was all on fire,
My being burned with a kindred flame
   And a passionate desire ;

With hands out-stretched and a beating heart
   I cried, though my lips were dumb,—
"Oh gleaming gates close not yet awhile!
   Oh, Wonderful Land, I come!"

But ere the cry could be heard above
   The glory turned to grey,
The gates were closed on my waiting soul,
   The light had passed away;
Then the darkness came and wrapped me round
   In misty clouds of night,
And I sighed as I sat in the silence dim,
   "Oh, when should I reach the light!"
Earth voices called me and wooed me soft,
   Yet panted my troubled breast,
As night by night in my fancy's dream
   I sank with the sun to rest.

But now I have entered that Wonderful Land,
   I have passed the golden gate;
No longer I stretch out weary hands,
   No longer I weep and wait;
The earth is lost in the clouds below,
   Behind me the dusky night,
My soul is soothed to a heavenly calm
   And filled with a holy light;
In a lovely dream I wander on,
   New wonders meet my gaze,

And close around me on either hand
　　Fresh bursts of glory blaze.

New floods of light are round me spread
　　As I climb each shining steep;
Above, are shim'ring waves of gold,
　　Beneath, an azure deep;
And on, and on, the clouds unroll,
　　The brightness quivering grows,
While answering to the spell divine
　　My spirit burns and glows,
But with a soft and gentle flame
　　That knoweth nought of pain,
And tears of joy break from mine eyes
　　As warm as summer rain.

And ever on my ravished ear
　　Low strains of music fall,
While from the golden heights above,
　　Sweet heavenly voices call;
My hands are clasped by hands unseen,
　　And ever by my side,
With footstep soft as falling snow,
　　I feel a presence glide;
And far away beyond the gold
　　I catch a fitful gleam
Of beings whiter than the light,
　　And fairer than a dream.

O lovely Land of light and song,
   Why must I haste away?
Why on thine ether hills so bright
   Could not my spirit stay?
Why must I wake on earth again?
   Why leave the sunset halls?
Why lose the mystic music sweet,
   The angel voice that calls?
I feel the cold world clasp me round,
   Earth voices round me play;
I wake, and the glory of my dream
   Hath turned to earthly grey.

But now as I walk the well-known paths,
   Or gaze on the evening sky,
A wondrous music is in my ears,
   Fair visions pass me by;
I hear the voices of flower and tree,
   The song of the waving grass,
The chant of the fleecy sun-born clouds
   As overhead they pass;
And bird and beast, and trickling stream,
   I know their secrets all;
From moor and plain, from hill and glen,
   A thousand voices call.

And then I turn to the haunts of men
   And tread through the crowded street,

And read with a vision grand and clear
 The faces of all I meet;
The souls look out from the human eyes
 And I see the longing vain,
The helpless cry of the weary mind,
 The want, and the aching pain;
I hear the throb and the lonely beat
 Of hearts that would fain be glad;
I catch the sound of the falling tear,
 The secret sigh of the sad.

So by the light of that Wondrous Land
 I walk the paths of earth;
I share the sorrow and the joy,
 The sadness and the mirth;
And soon again through the golden gates
 I shall pass the burning west,
Again beyond the crimson glow
 My eager soul shall rest;—
Ope wide your gates, gleam on, red sun!
 Stretch out, O burning band!
My heart beats on with an anxious throb
 Till I reach the Wonderful Land.

NATURE'S GREEN.

IF I were asked which I would have,
    Of all the colours seven,
Of all the shades from brown of earth
    Up to the blue of heaven,
My answer would be promptly this,—
    Of all the hues I've seen,
There's nothing like the soothing spell
    Which lies in Nature's Green.

The blue of summer sky is fair,
    But tires the gazing eyes ;
In flaunting red, and crimson deep,
    Too much of turmoil lies ;
So from their hot and glowing depths
    I turn with wearied mien,
And rest my strained and aching sight
    On Nature's quiet Green.

The purple hues of hill and flower
    Suggestive are of pain,

The anguish of the riven heart,
 And fields of newly slain ;
I turn from them with restless fear,
 No other tint, I ween,
Can give my soul a restful calm,
 Like Nature's living Green.

In yellow, gleams of anger blaze,
 And jealous embers glow ;
Bright orange tells of throbs of hate,
 A current deep and slow ;
From them I turn, and lift mine eyes
 Unto the leafy screen,
And thank kind Nature's gentle balm,
 Mid tender bowers of Green.

In sombre tints of grey and brown,
 Deep sorrows are entwined,
They show the melancholy moods
 And troubles of the mind ;
And when from these I would be free
 And happy thoughts would glean,
I muse amid the sunny shades
 Of Nature's waving Green.

It soothes the troubled mind to rest,
 And lures the spirit on ;
It gently lulls the anxious heart,
 Till care and pain are gone ;

So through all lands, and in all climes,
    Wherever I have been,
I turn from all the varied hues
    To Nature's living Green.

A PICTURE STORY.

"Yes, I've often heard of crystals,
    Into which if you but look,
You may read the past and future
    Plain as in a printed book.
'Only faith is needed,' say you,
    'To believe the sights we see;'
Well, my faith would move the mountains,
    And I oft have wished to be
Owner of some weighty secret,
    Watcher of some tragic scene,
Gazer on some heart's emotion,
    I myself, unknown, unseen;
Let me look, and on my honour
    I will tell you sure and true,
All that through your magic crystal
    Passes on in swift review."

FIRST PICTURE.

In idleness and loneliness,
    A lady sits at her window high

148

And gazes out on the rolling moors
    And up at the dark'ning evening sky ;
In bitterness and loneliness,
    While out in the distance far and gray,
Down into the dale beyond the moor,
    Her lover rides from her side away ;
In helplessness and loneliness,
    Though the morrow-morn, whate'er betide,
Beneath in the yew-tree-shaded church,
    Sir Hubert will claim her as his bride.

In helplessness and loneliness,
    For she loves, as only love the few,
Yet knows in her heart's deep consciousness,
    Her lover is neither strong nor true ;
In bitterest submissiveness,
    A father's mandate she must obey,
Fulfil the vow he has made for her,
    Long years ago on her natal day ;
In hopelessness and helplessness,
    To love, yet know there is no reply ;
To wed unloved, oh, the sting and shame,
    To live unloved ! it were best to die.

Oh, loneliness of loneliness,
    The lady creeps to her sleepless bed,
While wind-tossed boughs of the tall elm trees
    Wail their mournful dirges o'er her head.

" Here I pray you take your crystal
    If it show me scenes like this ;
Maidens on the eve of marriage
    Should be lost in dreams of bliss :
Why should fathers force their daughters
    On some swain who loves them not ?
Promise them when they are babies !
    Bah !   It makes my blood run hot !
What a life of gilded sorrow,
    Poverty, and secret pain !
Stop, don't take away your crystal,
    I would look yet once again ;
For perchance I there may gather
    Something that shall ease my heart,
And I fain would like to fathom
    How Sir Hubert plays his part."

SECOND PICTURE.

In bitterness and recklessness
    He rides full swiftly across the moor,
Till the bare wide wolds are left behind,
    And a smiling valley lies before ;
In helplessness and recklessness,
    For he loves, but not the Lady May,
Yet to save his house from want and woe,
    His truth and faith he must cast away ;

In faithlessness and recklessness
    Must sell his soul for the needed gold ;
For the *honour* of a noble house,
    A lie on the morrow must be told.

In agony of recklessness,
    He rides in haste down the grassy slope,
And tries to hide from his storm-tossed heart
    The years to come, void of love and hope ;
In bitterness and recklessness,
    For he knows that by the broken bridge,
Across the field with the hawthorn hedge,
    And over the narrow daisied ridge,
In hopefulness and joyfulness,
    He will see a lithesome figure stand,
And as he nears, in the evening dim,
    Will catch the wave of a tiny hand.

Oh, bitterness of bitterness !
    The one who waits him in trustful love ;
To-morrow morn, and the Lady May,
    And no help around, beneath, above.

"Surely, surely, through your crystal
    Never passed so strange a scene?
And I fain would think, but cannot,
    Such things, though they once have been,

Now are vanished and forgotten,
   Souls no longer can be sold,
Marriage vows no longer plighted
   At the filthy shrine of gold ;
I should like to think, but cannot,
   Men are men, who will not lie,
Dare not barter love and honour,
   Selling what no coin can buy ;
But again I look still further,
   For I long yet fear to see,
What shall be the sad deep purport
   Of the pictures yet to be."

THIRD PICTURE.

In sullenness and heedlessness,
   The beck glides on through the silent night,
With a burden once so sweet and warm,
   Which now it must safely hide from sight.
In carelessness and wantonness
   It flows o'er ripples of rich brown hair,
And stirs in its cold and thoughtless play
   The ribbon late tied with loving care.
In loneliness and silentness,
   A fair form lies in her reedy bed,
While stars look on from the quiet sky,
   And trees wave a requiem overhead.

In fearfulness and recklessness,
   Doth Sir Hubert's steed now homeward dash,
For a piercing scream is in his ears,
   Which came with sound of a sudden splash.
In wretchedness and recklessness
   His rider spurs him across the wold,
For the scream rings loud in his surging ears,
   And his blood is running chill and cold ;
In misery of wretchedness,
   He ever sees on the path ahead,
A form close wrapt in its garments dank,
   And a ghastly face, cold, blue, and dead.

Oh bitterness of bitterness,
   His love laid deep 'neath the silent flood,
And to-morrow morn when the Lady May
   Must clasp a hand that is stained with blood.

"Ah, me ! but I fear your crystal,
   Yet I know past all dispute,
That our wildest acts of passion
   In our loves have deepest root ;
That, when fear has made us cowards,
   And our sins start from their grave,
Oft we turn in maddest fury
   On the dearest thing we have ;
Bound in net of our own weaving
   We must break it through, alas

That, in breaking it, we often
　　Through worse sins seem called to pass ;
I must gaze again, for truly
　　I would see how this doth end ;
Sin on black base sin can only
　　Unto deeper darkness tend."

FOURTH PICTURE.

In fitfulness and dreariness,
　　The wind moans low round an ivied church,
As Sir Hubert and the Lady May
　　Step out through the rustic moss-grown porch ;
In haughtiness and stateliness,
　　The lady walks with a queenly tread,
Yet she knows for her all life holds dear,
　　All hope of happiness has fled ;
In stateliness and loneliness
　　She passes out to a martyr life,
Yet none can read in that pale still face
　　The aching heart of an unloved wife.

In haughtiness and wretchedness,
　　Sir Hubert walks with a heart of dread,
For on altar, bride, and chancel floor,
　　He sees but one face, cold, blue, and dead.
In ghastliness and awfulness,
　　What phantom now rises to his view ?

With raiment wet as her rich brown hair,
  And glazing eyes which were once so true?
Oh agony of agony,
  The phantom clutches his heart of dread;
A cry rings over the rolling moor,
  Sir Hubert lies with the ghost-love, dead.

In watchfulness and loneliness,
  In a convent cell, from night to day,
That a sin-stained soul may be forgiven,
  With pitying love doth a lady pray.

"Now I pray you take your crystal,
  And I never more will look,
Though it show me things more plainly
  Than in any printed book;
Yet I see from that last picture,
  How all sin doth make us weak,
How it dogs and tracks our footsteps,—
  Holds us when we fain would break
All the cords that bind and gird us
  In a loathsome, hideous chain;
Stands before us gaunt and ghastly,
  Though we turn to good again;
Shakes a hard remorseless finger,—
  Whispers to us, ' But for me,
All your life, with all its issues,
  Had been hopeful, brave, and free.'"

THE LAND OF ROMANCE.

You ask me why the poet oft
  Should leave the realm of fact,
And pass in silence the long way
  Of common toil and act.

You ask why he from town and street
  Should turn his inward glance,
To wander in a hazy dream
  Through lands of old Romance.

It is not that the poet scorns
  The present paths of life,
That he is blind to human need
  And deaf to human strife ;

But rather that in olden tale
  His poet eye can see,
How far beyond its meanest thought
  This present age might be.

So with intent of purpose good,
  He seeks the mystic past,
And laws of thought, and rules of time
  And space, aside are cast,

And in a realm, his own, and free
  To fancy's widest flight,
Whatever he may choose to place
  Is always true and right ;

And there, he need but wish, and lo,
  Up-rises to his will,
A valley fair, a flow'ry plain,
  A green or barren hill ;

Deep rivers glide at his command,
  And lakes are girdled round
With summer's greenest loveliness,
  Or lie in winter bound.

And under his almighty wand
  Dark forests gloom in dread,
Or copses smile, or silver birch
  Waves tenderly o'erhead ;

And skies grow dark with cloud and storm,
  Or gleam serenely bright,
Or burn in beauty as they fade
  From evening into night.

And at his need, in glade or wood,
  His castles fair may stand,
And cities rise in silent speed
  O'er his enchanted land ;

And knights and ladies, fancy wrought,
  Obey his gentle call,
And ride by sylvan stream or glen,
  Or tread through bower and hall.

And as on hoped-for fight intent
  They take their venturous way,
Strange chances happen, good and ill
  Change with the changing day.

And to their aid come unseen powers,
  And spirits round them fly,
And men and places come and go,
  Yet no one asketh why ;

For in that land, what is, is not,
  The false may real seem,
The good appear to fade and die
  Like some faint morning dream ;

But Presto, quick, the scene is changed,
  And from the dusty fight,
The hero issues to proclaim
  The *real* is the *right*.

So through these Knights of old Romance,
   And ladies grave or gay,
The poet speaks the truest thought
   That rules the present day.

The holy quest, the fearless fight,
   The knightly glory sought,
The courteous act, the valiant deed
   Which seem to end in naught ;

What are they but the poet's dream
   Of what to-day might be,
Were but the common mind more true
   To truest chivalry ?

So from the scenes of long ago,
   The times of past renown,
He brings an impulse that shall fire
   The honour of his own ;

And holy quest and valiant deed
   Be welcomed as of old,
Till noble fight, and stirring tale
   Of his own day be told,—

Till poets of the time to come
   May take a backward glance,
And see that e'en this present age
   Held something of Romance.

DREAMING AND WAKING.

Is living dreaming,
   Or is dreaming the true life ?
Is dying nothing
   But the ending of the strife ?—
For living, dreaming,
   Dying, which of them is best ?
Since waking, sleeping,
   We are none of us at rest.

Working and thinking
   All the long and anxious day,—
Kind evening calling,—
   Rest is sweet, we sometimes say ;
Tired of the pushing,
   Of the constant hum and tread,
Tired of the rushing
   Of the waters round our head ;
Gently and calmly
   Slumber-clouds do o'er us creep,
Till midnight falling
   Finds us in the land of sleep.

Through sleeping, waking
　　To another, swifter life ;
New scenes around us
　　Call new passions into strife ;
We act or suffer,
　　Pass through times of joy or pain,
Change, ever changing,
　　Till we sleep, or wake again.

Sleeping or waking,
　　Which is real, who can tell ?
Dreaming or waking,
　　In which region do we dwell ?
While working, thinking,
　　Waking hours are *life* we deem,
Till softly sleeping
　　All seems real that we dream.
And so with dying,
　　Is it but to sleep more sound,
Passing the dream-land
　　To a further realm beyond ?
Not re-awaking
　　In the world we know so well,
But passing onward
　　To a new one, who can tell ?

A PICTURE.

Yes, bound in the limits of gilded frame,
    There lieth a secret, caught
From the mystic dream of a poet's mind,
    And by artist's skill out-wrought ;
But a picture, small, yet it haunts the mind
    Like some oft-repeated tune,
Or the scents that float o'er the flow'ry fields
    On a balmy night in June.

'Tis a tree-clad rift in a mountain side,
    Where the winds have often passed,
Where the gaunt bare trunks and the twisted
      boughs
    Speak loud of the wintry blast ;
Where the rocks are bound by the serpent roots
    Which cling with a fervour grim,
While the torrent works them a certain fall
    Far down in the gorges dim.

And above the trees, all across the rift,
    There lieth a mountain mist,

Where the sun-drawn dews, and the snow-born
    breeze,
  Have met in the air and kissed ;
A mist that enshrouds in its silence deep
  All the secrets of the hill ;
No pathway, no crag, 'tis a vast abyss,
  Mysterious, dank, and chill.

But above the mist is a fair clear sky,
  And against the distant blue,
One snow-clad peak in the glorious light
  Stands full in the gazer's view :
So white, yet just tinged with a sunset gold,
  We scarce can assign its birth,
Shut out by the blue from the heaven above,
  Cut off by the mist from earth.

Did the poet soul, by the artist hand,
  Strive after an uttered speech,
Did he try to tell of the strain and stress
  His ideal high to reach ?
To show that afar in the future bright
  Was a height his feet might gain,
Through faults and failures, and struggles of years,
  Through shadow, and mist, and rain.

Or perhaps he meant that the poet's soul
  Dwells oft in a realm apart,

That the painter's skill and the poet's word
   Are speech from a lonely heart ;
That the noble thought and the high desire
   On the mountain peak have birth,
So near to heaven as to pierce the blue,
   Cut off by the mists from earth.

SONG OF THE CLOUDS.

Flecking the blue
  Of the vault above,
Forms ever new
  From pale ether wove,
We sing as we pass o'er the lower earth,
That world we have watched from its ancient birth.

We sing of time
  And its even flow,
Of ages past,
  Æons long ago,
For ere man stood forth on his wide domain,
We had lived, and died, and been born again.

We sing of earth,
  Of its changing face,
Its form of strength,
  And its lines of grace,
And we wrap it round in our loving arms,
While we deck it anew in fresh young charms.

We sing of man,
        Of his pain and woe,
    And weep to think
        Of his lot below,
Of the weary load of his mortal life,
Of his sin and sorrow and bitter strife.

        And in his ear
            We would sing this song,—
        Be true to God
            And in heart be strong,
Till like us ye mount to the realms above,
And your strife be hushed in eternal love.

        Strong hearts that burn
            In the eager breast,
        To sink like us
            In the gleaming west,
Press upward, onward, your race well run,
Till you soar past us, up beyond the sun,

        And we shall gaze
            From the nether sky,
        And smile to see
            Your bliss on high,
As ye bask in eternal glories bright,
And sing to us from your heaven of light.

QUESTIONINGS.

OH why, my soul, should thou so cling to life?
    'Tis but a toil and pain;
And why, when this dull round of earth is o'er,
    Dost long to live again?

Why search for knowledge, O my thirsty soul,
    When knowledge brings thee grief?
To strain so hard to reach the heart of all
    Sure brings thee no relief.

Why dost thou strive ideals high to gain?
    Why all thy thoughts refine?
When many sordid lives and earth-born souls
    Know less of care than thine.

Why dost thou long for love, my foolish soul,
    When love brings oft-time pain?
'Twere better far to miss the tempting cup
    Than bitter dregs to drain.

Why yearnest thou to wake the souls of men,
    To rouse them out of sleep ?
When thou thyself dost long for some repose,
    For death dost oft-times weep.

Why strive to leave a dull and foolish world
    The better for thy life ?
For thee to fight a countless armed host
    Were surely useless strife ?

Why dost thou fret because thou canst not solve
    The mystery of sin,
While those for whom thine anxious tears are shed
    Feel less of shame therein ?

No answer can I give thee, O my soul,
    No reason canst thou know ;
One word alone can help thee in the strife,
    'Tis this :—God made thee so.

All things that *live* to higher forms attain,
    All press to that far goal
When past and present, and things yet to be,
    Shall form one beauteous whole.

And when new worlds and brighter skies appear,
    Where wouldst thou have thy place ?
'Mid those who lagged behind, who feared the
        road ?
    Or foremost in the race ?

And soul, my soul, when thou at last shalt leave
    This planet far behind,
Wouldst thou be ready for broad floods of light,
    For boundless realms of mind?

Then press thou on though anxious tears and sighs,
    And hours of pain, be thine ;
Content to bear the hunger and the smart
    Which prove thy life Divine.

THE GODS.

Shut in, bound down, O human heart divine,
    Thou cri'st with an awful cry,
"Where is my God? Why doth he hide from men
    While faiths are born and die?"

"Where is my God?" The cry comes echoing down
    From out the ages dim,
While mountain top and lonely forest glade
    Send forth the suppliant hymn.

In ancient times, when earth was fair and young,
    Men sought Thee far and wide,
Stretched out weak hands, and bent the lowly knee,
    As for their God they cried.

They sought Thee midst the glittering stars of night,
    In mountain, stream, and sea,
While morn and eve the pale blue smoke arose
    From altars raised to Thee.

And when the flames leaped ambient in the air,
    And struggling victim died,
Men watched and waited, could not find Thee there,
    Though on Thy Name they cried.

And some there were who took the stones of earth,
    And trees which Thou hadst made,
And fashioned them with rude and rapid skill,—
    " These be our Gods !" they said.

And still the cry rang ever through the air,
    " God cannot thus be known,
He dwelleth not in what our hands have made,
    In blocks of wood and stone."

And others turned to cast a loving eye
    On flower, and stream, and tree,
Heard voices call them from the lake's still deep,
    And from the restless sea.

And seeking Thee, they peopled hill and plain,
    And fount and cavern dim ;
Gods dwelt within the leafy curtained grove,
    And forest arches dim.

And temples rose, and altars decked with flowers
    Sent up the sacred smoke,
As shouts of praise to Nature's sovereign power
    The morning stillness broke.

And yet the cry rang ever through the air,
    "God cannot dwell in these,
They fade and change, they die and pass away,
    As dies the evening breeze."

O seeking souls, where shall they find their God,
    How end the anxious quest?
Where shall they turn their weary, thirsty hearts
    For hope, and love, and rest?

Some loved to think on feats by man enwrought,
    On art, and strength, and skill,
And framed them Gods like unto human-kind,
    Gods who could think and will.

And grander far the temples now they raise,
    And richer gifts they gave,
And on their human gods they called aloud,
    To hear, and bless, and save.

The Gods came down from off their sacred hill,
    They sought the battle's din,
They walked with men, shared the same pleasures
      wild,
    And shared, alas, the sin.

And still the cry rang ever through the air,—
    "These Gods! they are but clay,
They sin like us, they love and hate like us,
    Like us they must decay."

And some stood forth, and cried with calm, still
    voice,
  "List now to us!" they said;
"There are no Gods! Fear neither good nor ill;
    Hark you, the Gods are dead!

"They could not save you from the ills of life,
    Or give you rest and peace;
Come now to us, drink deep of wisdom's well,
    Thus shall your conflict cease.

"Take good and ill, the chance that comes to all,
    Nor fret yourselves in vain;
Be more than Gods; despise earth's sweetest joys,
    And trample on its pain.

"Unmoved and steadfast, like a mighty rock
    'Mid ocean's wild unrest,   .
Untouched by sorrow, careless of success,
    Ye shall be truly blest."

But still the cry rang louder through the air:
    "Without our Gods we die;
Cold, cold the breath of your philosophies,
    Cold, though so pure and high.

"It falls upon us like an icy blast,
    Piercing, and clear, and chill;
No heart, no hope, no tender touch of love
    Our hungry souls to fill.

"Our hearts are human, and they will not rest,
　　We love, and sin, and die;
We want a God to pity and forgive,
　　A God to hear our cry."

O'er all the world rang still the old refrain,
　　"Where doth God hide his face?
We search in vain, stretch eager hands in prayer,
　　To find His dwelling-place."

Till in some minds was born the awful thought,
　　God hates what He hath made;
And men, struck dumb beneath an iron fate,
　　Shrank trembling and afraid.

How could they charm the hard, relentless laws,
　　How stay the vengeful stroke?
The Gods but laughed; up there beyond the blue
　　They mocked at human folk;

And cruel, bitter grew the love-lost hearts,
　　When Gods must be appeased,
And wild and awful grew their sacred rites,
　　Like to the Gods they pleased.

Or if in quiet solitude afar
　　Some lonely soul should stray,
And wrapt in contemplation deep and calm
　　To Thee should humbly pray;—

Yet eager longings stir his soul at times,—
    "My God, I want Thee near,
I search for Thee, stretch hand and heart to Thee,
    But cannot feel Thee here."

So still the cry rang ever through the air,
    The aching, bitter cry,
"Where is our God ? Why doth He hide from men,
    While creeds are born and die ? "

God came to earth, He trod the streets and ways,
    He shared the common life,
He passed through human sorrow, human joy,
    Through want, and pain, and strife.

And *Father* was the name that softly fell
    Upon the listening ear,
As men looked up in new-born hope and trust,
    And breathed once more in prayer,

Father ;—and like a gentle breeze at eve
    Hearts sank to quiet rest ;
A Father God—mankind might be at peace
    Upon His shelt'ring breast.

But many turn away in sadness still
    And seek for God elsewhere ;
They search 'mid laws of nature, cause, and force,
    But do not find Him there.

"O great First Cause, come, show Thyself to men,
  Disclose Thy secret life,
Why all this pain, why all this wrong and woe?
  Why all this war and strife?"

And still the cry rings often through the air,
  Hearts struggle for the light ;
And shall the souls that yearn to see Thy face
  Remain in clouds of night ?

Nay sure for all shall come the longed-for dawn,
  The day of liberty,
When through the striving of their wild unrest
  Their God at last they see ;—

When far behind them lie the plains of earth,
  And to their spirit eyes
A vaster sphere, a clearer, purer light,
  A higher life arise ;

And a new cry shall ring through sunlit air,
  And o'er the crystal sea,
And down the aisles where countless lives to come
  Wait in the " Yet to be,"

O God, the centre and the source divine
  Of all man's common lot,
Thy ministries the gracious earth fulfilled,
  And yet we knew Thee not ;—

We must have met Thee in the lane and street,
 And passed Thee in our kin,
And that we would not, could not, yield to Thee
 Is now our deepest sin ;—

Forgive us, Lord ; and in the life to be
 Make us more truly wise ;
Teach us though late to find Thee everywhere,
 Open our spirit eyes.

M

A CASTLE IN THE AIR.

A CASTLE, yes, I built it
   On yielding plains of air,
And clear above the purple hills
   Shone its foundations fair.

It stood on aspirations,
   And ardent dreams of youth,
And true or false, its basement stones
   Were laid in Love of Truth.

Its walls were white and perfect,
   Upbuilt of noble thought,
Of pure resolves, or impulse keen
   In action to be wrought.

And round about the portals,
   And o'er the casements high,
Were carved the fancies light and free
   That flash, then hurry by.

And curves of arching splendour
  On pillared height upborne,
Like beauty based on righteousness,
  Its halls and courts adorn.

Its turrets !   Ah, the turrets,
  Hid in the light sublime
Which still recedes, as year by year
  We mount the steps of time,—

Yet clear against the sunset,
  Or caught by morning beam,
At times its pinnacles and spires
  Would swift and sudden gleam.

And aye within the castle
  Was refuge for distress,
And wide its gates for ever stood
  To want and helplessness.

And none who sought its shelter
  But found some heart relief,
Some inspiration to the right,
  Some joy to sweeten grief.

And where is now the castle
  Once built on plains of air ?
Are all its walls in ruin laid,
  And lost its turrets fair ?

Nay, though in the foundation
   Were stones that proved untrue,
And though some walls have crumbled quite,
   And some are broken through,

And though some lines of beauty
   Have lost their early grace,
And dusky clouds of hopes betrayed
   Some of its towers efface ;

For fairer are the ruins,
   And lovelier in decay,
Than sordid walls and low-set eaves
   Of common house of clay.

And round the broken arches
   The kindly ivy clings,
And from amid the fallen stones
   The purple heart'sease springs ;

And long past faults and failures
   Now lend a chastened grace,
And flowers of everlasting bloom
   The wrecks of time efface.

And still the castle standeth
   On yielding plains of air,
And clear above the purple hills
   Shine its foundations fair.

THE OUTER COURTS.

IF thou wouldst keep thine inner chambers holy,
  Then in the outer courts no dust must fall,
Nor stranger voices of a worldly traffic
  Within the precincts of thy temple call.

Holy of Holies, home of the Eternal,
  A sacred shrine thy heart can only be,
If the broad pavement of thy speech and action
  From sordid lust and passions false be free.

Guard then the threshold, make the courtyard worthy
  To be the entrance to thy holy place,
Then shalt thou know the strange and mystic rapture
  Of those who see Jehovah face to face.

"GOD IS IN HIS HOLY TEMPLE."

In calm sublime
Of ancient time
Thy glory dwelt within the sacred shrine ;
From man apart,
A lonely heart
And the sad splendour of repose were Thine ;
Nor day nor night
'Mid the soft light
That veiled Thy presence in the Holy Place,
No struggling word
Of prayer was heard,
Nor turned to Thee one wistful human face.

When glow of dawn
Broke with the morn
Across the beauty of a waking world,
Within Thy shade
No sunbeam played,
And still Thy purple curtain hung unfurled ;

And when the day
Passed calm away
No star lit up the mystic chamber dim,
Where vast and lone,
The nameless One,
Thy presence dwelt between the cherubim.

No fleecy cloud
Above Thee bowed,
Nor bent for Thee the arch of sapphire blue,
Nor rippling trill
Of bird or rill
Ere broke the stillness of Thy glory through ;
No breath of flowers
In summer hours
Made the lone places of Thine altar sweet,
And never more
Across Thy floor
Rang the glad patter of the children's feet.

Beyond Thy gate,
In love or hate
Passed the frail tenants of Thy chosen land,
Yet Thou alone
Hast never known
The tender touch or clasp of human hand.
No soul in grief
Ere sought relief
Within the shadow of Thy lone retreat,

And never tear
Of joy or fear
Dimmed the gold lustre of Thy mercy-seat.

If songs of mirth
Woke the glad earth,
For Thee rose but the incense of the feast,
And grief for sin
Thy house within
Glowed on the crimson hand of white-robed priest ;
And when at last
Life's journey past
No quiet form was at Thy footstool laid,
Nor mourner's tread
Brought the loved dead
Within the coldness of Thy deathless shade.

Ah ! great Unknown,
Hast Thou alone
To know no change throughout thine onward years ?
'Twere better fate
Beyond Thy gate
To live the progress wrought through smiles and tears ;
Yea doth God change?
Ah ! passing strange
That Thy great Temple shrines must fade away,
Ere Thou couldst find
In human kind
The changes of a new and fairer day ;

And never more
Shall Temple door
Close Thee in silent solitude again,
But wide and free
Thy Life shall be,
Changed in the ever changing thoughts of men.

SONGS FROM MACPHERSON'S "OSSIAN."

SONGS sung in other days ring sadly sweet
   Amid the poems of a later time,
And from the past, long echoes oft repeat
   The wind-tossed harpings of far northern clime ;
And whether by Macpherson's fancy wrought,
   Or sung by Ossian in fair Selma's Hall,
These simple songs from Odin's land are caught,
   And sentiment, not history, recall.

CONLATH AND CUTHONA.

      The wind blows chill
Through the wide halls of Selma* ; in the blast
The shield of Fingal echoes 'mid the gloom,
And Ossian, wakeful in the tempest, starts
From fragrant couch, for, sighing through the storm,
A voice comes far from o'er the curling wave,
And on the pathway of the gull, there flies
The sound of woe.

      " Who art thou, son of night,
Whose voice comes dirge-like through my father's
  hall ?
Was it a voice ?

      Or was it but the sound
Of days that are no more, the former times
Which often gleam like sun at eventide
Upon my sinking day ?

      The feeble sleep ;
The wind is in my hall, and on its wing
Come noises of the chase, of horn and hound,
Across the level plain.

   * Selma, the Palace of Fingal.

"Was it a voice?
Or doth the hand of Fingal touch once more
His moon-beam shield, where high it hangs above
His glitt'ring arms, till my fond mem'ry wakes
To tread the field of war, where o'er the slain
The heroes feast, and high the sounding harp
Of Ullin pours the fun'ral song for those
Who sleep beneath the stones.
     Was it a voice?
Or was it but the wind?
      And who is this

That like a wreath of grey and shrouded mist
Creeps tall from out the dusk across my floor?
'Tis Conlath, son of Morni, his the form,
But dim as cloud when the long rain-swept day
Is settling on the sea.
      Why comest thou
From off thy Hill of Ghosts?
      What seekest thou
Of Ossian in the night?"

GHOST OF CONLATH.

Sleeps the sweet voice of Cona* in his hall,
 And dry the grasses rustle in the breeze;
On the far rocks the broken waters fall,
 And snow-white billows ride the curling seas.

   * Voice of Cona, Ossian.

But Conlath wanders in the trackless night,
  And ghost-like, ever in the driving gale,
He melts like cloud before the beam of light,
  Or walks in mist when evening skies grow pale.

Fair was Cuthona, daughter of the sun,
  Her hair like beam of glory in the west,
Her voice the song of bird when day is done,
  Her eyes the blue of mountain lakes at rest.

Fleet was the maid when hunting on the hills,
  And Toscar saw,—ah, weep the ill-sped day;
Hush your soft murmurs, oh ye mossy rills,
  For black the night that stole my love away.

Three days he feasted in her father's halls;
  For him was spread the couch, flowed forth the song,
Then swift he bore the maid from Mora's walls,
  And far they sailed the rocky seas along.

Wrathful I heard, then sought Ithona's* isle,
  Where angry waves beat round the desert rock,
Then came bold Toscar of the wintry smile
  With his friend Fercuth to the deadly shock.

  * Ithona, a desert island of Scandinavia.

Fierce clang the shields, and sharp along the blast
   The blows of battle drive the piercing sand,
Bold Toscar sinks, and Fercuth down is cast,
   And Conlath lies upon the blood-red strand.

Then comes the fair Cuthona, lovely maid,
   Pale from her rock, as moonbeam on the wave ;
Low is her voice, as streams that sink and fade
   Within the hollow of some mountain cave :

"Dead art thou, Conlath, son of Morni, thou,
   Thy beauty wasted in its early noon ;
No more to thee the fallen foe shall bow,
   No more for thee the white Feast of the Moon.

" But round thy head Cuthona weeps in pain,
   As here thy follow'rs strew the silent shore,
Weeps for the love that never comes again,
   And for the days of beauty now no more.

" For thee alone Cuthona's tears arise,
   For true to thee her every thought of love ;
For thee her heart bled, as here now her eyes
   Weep these salt tears, thy clay-cold breast above.

"True was my love when through the storm and mist
 Bold Toscar bore me from my father's halls ;
Speak to me, lips so blue that I have kissed,
 'Tis the lone voice of thy Cuthona calls."

Then far across the sea to Fingal borne
 Came news of slain on lone Ithona's isle,
And swift from out the gateways of the dawn
 The heroes came to build the mossy pile ;

And there beside the blue and surging wave
 The fair Cuthona with her Conlath sleeps,
But unremembered is that distant grave,
 And, save the sea, none ever round it weeps.

Alas for them, though built the narrow tomb,
 No bard sailed forth great Fingal's chiefs among ;
For them no harp was struck to chant their doom,
 Or tell their love in low and mournful song.

Rise, voice of Cona ! Ossian's voice arise !
 Why sleeps he and his friends without their fame ?
Wake, son of Fingal, let the list'ning skies
 Catch the sweet echo of Cuthona's name.

N

Tell to the winds the tale of Conlath's woe,
 Sing how he fell on far Ithona's shore,
That in the narrow house, his form laid low,
 His ghost may leave the Hill of Shades no more.

Then rang the harp to mighty Conlath's praise,
 To fair Cuthona by the sounding wave,
Where now they sleep the sleep of other days,
 And clouds sail swan-like o'er their quiet grave.

COMALA.

THE DAUGHTERS OF MORNI.

"The chase is over and there falls
No sound in Ardven but the torrent's roar,
And moan of rising wind.
            Night comes at last,
Grey night along the plain, so grey and dim,
That deer at Cona's stream appears as bank
Of mossy turf, till swift he bounds away
With light between his horns ; and faces strange
Look down from clouds of Crona, these the signs
Of hero's death ; the king of shields is fallen,
And Caracul prevails."
            So softly spake
The " Brightness of a Sunbeam," fair-haired maid,
And Melilcoma, or "soft rolling eye,"
Daughters of Morni, where they sat to watch
Comala as she broods in grief alone
Upon her silent rock.   And then they sang :—

Oh rise, Comala, from thy rock,
Fair daughter, rise in tears,

The lover of thy youth is low,
 E'en now his ghost appears.

Dim faces of the other times
 Look out from Crona's cloud,
And meteor plays amid the horns
 Of deer by water bowed ;

See Fingal prone before the foe,
 His ghost is on our hills,
And shout from Caracul's great host
 The dreamy distance fills ;

And here Comala sits forlorn,
 Two grey dogs by her side,
Her red cheek rests upon her arm,
 Her hair floats free and wide ;

Her blue eyes turn towards the field
 Where lights of battle burn,
The field from which with paling night
 She waits her love's return.

Daughter of Sarno, rise in tears,
 Give thy faint soul its wings ;—
And now from off her lonely rock
 The Love of Fingal sings.

COMALA.

Rise, moon, thou changeful daughter of the clouds,
 And look through tears from out thy dusky sky,
And light the path by which the fleeting ghost
 Of Fingal, my true love, is passing by.

Or rather, let that meteor strange and dread,
 Which leads our fathers through the gloom of night,
Show me the way where on the bloody field
 My hero lies amid the crimson fight.

Like coming of the morning shone my love,
 Like cloud of glory from the golden east
Shone Fingal, when afar in Inistore
 He sat with heroes at my father's feast.

What wonder that Comala's heart was torn,
 That out upon the quiv'ring wings of love
My soul should pass from out my longing breast,
 And near him like a ghost should live and move?

Strong suitors oft had told their passion's flame,
 Hidallan wooed me in my father's hall,
But till my Fingal came, a beam of light,
 Had I passed thoughtless through the sighs of all.

I saw, I loved, and for my lover's sake,
 Clad in bright arms, I took the spear and shield,

And followed on the skirts of gloomy war
   Where red it rolled across the trodden field.

Then silent all my woman's tender fears,
   I looked unmoved when bleeding heroes fell;
Before me moved the star of all my days,
   I saw, I loved, I followed, all was well.

Ah, why did fierce Hidallan's prying eyes
   Beneath the arms disclose the blushing maid?
And so the passion of my love and youth
   Was to great Combal's son at once betrayed;

Then why did news of battle break the bliss
   That fell across the pathway of my life,
And let the future snatch from me the day
   Of joy, when I should be great Fingal's wife?

But Fingal promised he would come ere night,
   I wait his coming from the bloody field,
I watch for sunshine of his golden hair,
   For steel-blue lightning of his spear and shield.

But who comes here from out the mist and gloom?
   Is it Hidallan? Thou, my worse than foe!
"What tidings hast thou from the fight of kings?
   What dismal message, cursèd son of woe?"

HIDALLAN.

Dwell thou gloomy mist of Crona
  On the pathway of the king,
Let no more his ghostly footsteps
  To my mind his image bring.

Fallen is the mighty Fingal,
  See the scattered battle reel,
Severed all the bands asunder,
  Hushed the clang of echoing steel.

Not beside the moonlit Carun*
  Do the heroes build his tomb,
But to Ardven's lonely whiteness
  Has the chief of warriors come.

There they lay his shield and dagger,
  There they rear the mossy stones,
There the tears in mist are falling,
  There the wind of sorrow moans ;—

While I hastened to Comala,
  Maiden where thou sit'st forlorn,
For thy beauty and thy sadness
  All my heart in me is torn.

Blow, O gentle breezes, lightly
  Lift her locks as thick they lie,

* Carun, the river Carron.

Let me see her cheek rose-tinted,
    Though through tears, her star-like eye ;

Let me see her white arms gleaming
    Through her long and dusky hair,
Soon on me, in days returning,
    Sweet shall smile the maiden fair.

COMALA.

And why, Hidallan of the mournful tale,
    Hast thou come hither with thy news so dread ?
I might have hoped awhile my love's return,
    And now my soul must mourn him midst the dead.

I might have seen him on the distant rock,
    A tree to me his image might appear,
And wind from off the misty pine-topped hill
    Have been his horn low sounding in mine ear.

Confusion track thy footsteps o'er thy plains,
    And few thy steps be to thy narrow grave ;
And when on Caracul black death descends
    May there be none to pity, none to save !

What matters it if by the Carun's flood
    Or lone on Ardven lies my hero low ?
Like thunder in the battle was his voice,
    His foot as fleet as is the desert roe.

His hair was like the mist upon the hill,
    And curling golden in the mid-day sun;
White was he as the snow on Ardven seen,
    And bright as bow in heaven when showers are done.

Sons of the grave, let me behold my love,
    He left me smiling at the woody chase,
He promised to return ere fall of night,
    And now Comala sees no more his face.

He promised, yet he comes not at my call,
    Comala waits, my love, thy widowed bride,
Oh, let thy hand fall softly on my hair,
    And draw me once again thy heart beside.

Ah, there he comes, his crowd of ghosts among,
    And dost thou come to please me or affright?
Take me, my love, to thy lone cave of rest,
    There would I meet thee in the shades of night.

I hear his voice, it comes from off the hills,
    I see him ghost-like, but I do not fear;
I fade, I die, beyond the Gate of Shells
    My love shall find his own Comala near.

FINGAL.

Ye bards raise the song
For the war that is o'er,

For Caracul fled
To return nevermore,
And Comala arise, shake the fear from thy breast,
And come to the cave of my rest.

He sets on the heath
In the far distant night,
No more by our streams
Shall his eagles alight,
Then Comala arise, haste, oh haste to my breast,
And come to the cave of my rest.

Why silent the rock ?
And I hear not her voice,
O bards, raise the song,
Bid Comala rejoice,
Bid Comala arise, chase the fear from her breast,
Bid her come to the cave of my rest.

Alas ! by the rock
She lies silent in death,
And out on the air
Floats her quivering breath.
And as cold as the snow is the chill of her breast,
And empty the cave of my rest.

Hidallan, on thee
Is the shame and the woe,
Henceforward thy name
Shall be stranger and foe.

'Twas the shock of thy lies chased the life from her
    breast,
And darkened the cave of my rest.

    No more in my halls
        Shalt thou feast at my board,
    My foes shall not flee
        From thy treacherous sword,
I hate thee for ever, spurn thy thought from my
    breast,
For cold is the cave of my rest.

    The winds lift her hair
        From the white of her brow,
    It waved in the chase
        In its beauty, but now
It is trailing unmoved o'er the snow of her breast,
And bare is the cave of my rest.

    Ye bards, raise her name
        On the far driving wind;
    Ye bards, chant her praise,
        Till the pathway she find
To the hall of the dead, for not now on my breast
Shall she sleep in the cave of my rest.

    But when I sit lone
        By the low sounding rills,
    Return, O my love,
        From the mist of thy hills,

Lay thy white hand in mine, and thy head on my
    breast,
Oh, come to the cave of my rest.

BARDS.

Roll, streamy Carun, roll in floods of joy,
    For far the sons of battle all are fled ;
No more their steeds shall splash the curdling foam,
    No more their eagles o'er thy fountains spread.

The sun will now ascend from hills of joy,
    And set again in quiet shades of peace,
For from the land the sons of battle flee,
    And clang of spear and distant war-cry cease.

Roll, streamy Carun, roll in floods of joy,
    From off the hill rings out the horn of chase,
Rise, spirits of the dead, as o'er the sea
    Fade out the white wings of the hated race.

Then, Carun, hush thy song ! no flood of joy
    Break now thy green and mossy rocks along,
Sad be thy flow by some low reedy shore,
    And sad the burden of thy heavy song.

Weep for Comala, pale beside her rock,
    Short was her pathway to the narrow tomb,
Swift was the shaft that pierced her tender heart
    And sent her spirit on the path of gloom.

Daughter of Sarno, soon thy father's ghost
   Shall meet thee in the far-off Hall of Shells;
While here thy lover shall lament thy fall,
   Here lone for thee the mighty Fingal dwells.

See! meteors gleam around the beauteous maid,
   See! from above white moonbeams lift her soul;
From out the clouds her fathers' faces bend,
   And wreaths of glory round her softly roll.

When shall her voice be heard amid the rocks?
   When shall the gleam of her white hand arise?
The maids shall seek thee on the windy heath,
   But never catch the light from thy blue eyes.

And by the rock shall Fingal call thy name,
   And wait thy coming by the moon-lit stream,
And thou shalt float at times on wings of peace
   And pass across the beauty of his dream;

Thy voice shall whisper in the breeze of night,
   Thy hand fall softly on his golden hair,
Then sweet shall be the visions of his rest,
   And calm will be his soul when thou art there.

     Gleam meteors round the maid
     And moonbeams lift her soul,
While round her head the mists of glory roll.

SONGS OF SELMA.

Soft evening steals
On Morven, on the bare and wind-swept halls
Of Fingal, and the warriors long since passed,
Her voice as gentle and serenely calm
As is the star which stately in the west
Mounts high from peak to peak, and ridge to ridge
Of the far silent hills, till clear above
It sails in beauty o'er the level plain,
Where stormy winds are laid.

          From the lone glen
The murmur of the torrent scarce disturbs
Th' enchanted air, nor yet the circling waves
Which mount the shining rocks.

          O'er drowsy fields
The flies hum feebly on their lazy wing,
While in the hall, where dusky shadows creep,
Comes Morven's chief, like column of white mist,
So grey and ghostlike in the gloom ; and there
The heroes who in days of other years
Had bowed and swayed in combat, like the grass

Which bends and whistles in the gales of spring,
When swift before them fly the mist-white clouds
Which cradle in the west, are shadowy seen
Around the silent hearth.
                 And there the Bards
Of Selma, as upon the Feast of Shells,
With harp and song they raised the lovely tale
Of Shilric and Vinvela, and the days
Before the long-haired sons of Comhal* passed
In shadow to the narrow house; for there
Is grey-haired Ullin, mighty in his strength;
And Alpin of the tuneful voice; and sweet
Minona, daughter of complaint, and white
As sea-gull's under-wing.
                Step forth, O maid,
In beauty radiant as the silver moon
When fair she rides upon the rippled sea!
And sad as low wind through the distant pines
Minona sang her song of love and death.

Why weeps fair Colma on the hill of storms,
And pours her plaint to the long piteous rain?
Why streams her hair along the whistling wind
And bare her arm to the sharp driving hail?

The torrent pours in thunder down the glen,
And clouds fly ghost-like o'er the shad'wy plain,

---

* Comhal, the father of Fingal.

The sea afar roars round its rifted rocks,
While Colma sings forlorn upon the hills :—

" Shine out, white moon, and show my love the way
To where I watch beside the mossy stream ;
Stars of the west, arise, and lend your light,
I wait his coming though the night be late.

" Ye waters, hush you down the steep grey rock,
Ye winds, sing low among the bending reeds,
And let him hear my voice across the plain,
I call and listen though the night be late.

" Where dost thou wander on the moon-lit hills ?
Across what path doth thy long shadow fall ?
Send me some word from thy lone hiding-place
And I will hasten, though the night be late.

" Alone and sad I listen for thy horn,
Watch for thy hound to tell thy footstep near,
But Salgar comes not, haste, oh, haste, my love,
Though stars are waning, and the night grows late.

" Ah ! who are these so silent on the plain ?
Cold, cold their breasts as ice on fountain spray ;
Ghosts from the halls beyond the Gate of Shells
Who come to haunt me when the night is late ?

" Brother and Lover, dead in mortal feud,
The dews of night fall on you cold and chill,

And now for you awaits the narrow house,
While I must wander, though the night be late.

" Fallen, O my Salgar, lovely in thy prime,
Thy hair a beam from out the golden east,
Strong was thine arm, now in the dust laid low,
While here I mourn thee, as the night grows late.

" Speak once again, thy voice, though faint and weak,
Will reach thy Colma from the far-off land ;
I see thee ghost-like in the mist and rain
My tears have gathered, as the night grows late.

" My life a dream, no more shall Selma's halls
See Colma shine amid her daughters white,
For here I rest beside the sounding rock,
And weep my Salgar, though the night be late."

And so Minona ceased, and like the moon
When fast she hides her face before a shower,
With eyes of tears she faded out of sight,
As Ullin took the harp, and sang the song
Of Alpin mourning for the slain :—

My tears are for the dead, my voice for those
Who fall like saplings in the spring-tide gale ;
Who pass like foam upon a summer sea,
Or fade like flowers new burst, before the storm.

O

For thee, great Morar, car-born son of strength,
Swift as the roe in desert was thy foot,
Thy sword in battle, lightning in a field,
Thy voice the sound of waters midst the rocks.

Fierce was thy wrath in battle with the foe,
And many fell beneath thy flashing arm;
But when returning to thy father's halls,
Bright was thy face as sunshine after rain.

Yet thou wast slain, and o'er thine earthly bed
Four stones with mossy heads uprear them straight,
And on thy grave a tree with scarce a leaf,
And long dry grass, which whistles in the wind.

But who comes here, his head all white with age,
And leaning on his staff in lonely grief?
Who but thy father, Morar of the hills,
Who mourns in thee his star of glory set.

"Morar, my son, the hope of all my days,
Thy father bends above thy narrow house,
With broken voice like wind in blasted pine
I sing thy praises ere I fade in death.

"No mother hast thou to lament thy fall,
For dead, long dead, is she that brought thee forth;
Vanished thy sister, sweet Minona white,
I only mourn thee ere I fade in death.

"No wife hadst thou, no son will bear thy name,
Oh, Morar, greatest of the sons of men !
But to the years thy fame shall pass in song,
As now I praise thee ere I fade in death.

"Tall was thy form when hunting on the hills,
Thy hair like ruddy gold in evening sun ;
Thine arms white as the narwhal's glitt'ring bone,—
Oh, how to praise thee ere I fade in death.

"Alas, my son, slain in thy rosy youth,
'Twas thine to lay me in my narrow grave ;
'Twas thine to build the stones upon my tomb,
And mourn my going when I fade in death.

" 'Tis not for eve to weep the purple dawn,
Or winter to bemoan the coming spring ;
'Tis not for age to sing of youth laid low,—
Yet here I mourn thee ere I fade in death.

" No more thy voice shall ring along the morn,
Thy footstep echo through my lonely halls,
But deep and far beyond the Gate of Shells
Thy shade awaits me when I fade in death."

         Then rose the grief of all,
But most the bursting sigh of Armin filled
The shaken air, and Carmor at his side
The chief of echoing Galmal heard in pain ;—

" Why bursts the sigh of Armin ?   Is there cause
For thee to mourn ?   The song comes soft and low
With music sweet to melt and please the soul,
Like the soft mist that rising from the lake
Pours on the silent vale, or like the dew
Within the green flower's cup, let but the sun
Arise in his full strength, and lo they both
Are vanished like to smoke.
             Why art thou sad
O Armin, chief of Gorma ? "
                And once more
On evening breeze through Selma's halls there rose
A song of other years.

Ay, sad I am, nor small my cause of woe,
And thou, great Carmor, hast not lost a son,
Thy daughter shines in beauty in thy halls,
While I am left to tread my years alone.

Rise, winds of Autumn, blow along the heath !
Streams roar, and tempests tear my groves of oak !
Walk through the riven clouds, O pale-faced moon !
Bring back the night when I was left alone ;

When Arindal my son of glory fell,
And Daura, sweeter than the breathing gale ;
My son ! thy shield a red cloud in a storm,
My daughter, fairer than the rising moon.

And Armar came, he asked for Daura's love,
Nor was he long refused, the strong in war;
Oh, why did Erath hear, his foe till death,
Who waited vengeance for a brother slain?

Foul Erath came disguised like son of sea,
And white his locks like foam upon the wave,
And calm his brow, as from his bounding skiff
With gentle voice he called the lovely maid.

" Fairest of women! lonely maiden, hear!
There stands a rock not distant in the sea,
And by the tree whose red fruit shines afar
Thy lover waits thy coming on the shore."

She went; she called on Armar; naught replied
But the lone echo of the barren rock;
While Erath fled with laughter to the land,
And Daura lifted high her voice and wept.

"My Father! listen to this broken cry!
O Arindal, my brother, haste to me!
And Armar, my beloved! is there none
To save me from the cruel hungry wave?"

Her voice came faint from far across the sea,
And Arindal, descending from the chase,
Surprised fierce Erath on the sounding shore,
And bound him to a tall and lonely tree.

And fast his skiff was bounding o'er the tide
When Armar came in wrath, and swift his shaft
Sank in thy heart, O Arindal my son,
And left me here to tread my years alone.

For Erath wast thou slain ; upon the rock
Around thy sister's feet ran red thy blood ;
While Armar plunged in the loud angry sea
To save his Daura from the wave or die ;

When came a sudden blast from off the hill,
And Armar sank amid the trailing weeds,
While on the rock my daughter's voice grew weak,
As through the night I watched and wept alone.

What could her father do ?   From my lone shore
I saw her by the faint beam of the moon ;
Loud was the wind, the rain beat on the hills,
As there I wandered in my grief alone.

The morning came, her voice, now scarcely heard,
Died like an evening breeze amid the grass,
Till by her brother's side she sank in death,
And I was left to tread my years alone.

Gone is my strength in war, no son is left ;
My pride of women fallen in her prime ;
And Armin, last of all his fated race,
Is left to tread his last sad years alone ;

But when the storms lift high the surging wave,
I sit by night upon the sounding shore,
And gaze through tears upon the fatal rock
That saw me left to tread my years alone,

And there, lit by the setting moon, I see
The ghosts of my two children wander white ;
They talk together, but their eyes ne'er seek
The further shore where I must mourn alone,

Will none of you have pity, O ye chiefs
And heroes who abide in Fingal's hall !
Yea I am sad, nor small my cause of woe,
Since I am left to tread my years alone.

                              Then died the voice,
The harp of Ullin faded into mist,
While from the shadows of the moonlit plain
The hall and heroes vanished as a cloud,
And with a sigh that trembled into tears
The songs of Selma ceased.

THE MAID OF LULAN.

"BREEZE of the valley, wanderer unseen,
Thou bender of the thistle's purple head,
Why hast thou left mine ear ? I hear no more
The distant roar of streams ; no sound of harp
Comes to me from the rock.
     Malvina, rise,
Thou huntress of broad Lutha's plain,
Call back from off his hill of cloudy mist
The spirit of the bard, and bid him sing
A song of other days."
      Then sweeping soft
Across the trembling strings, the strain arose
Of deeds of olden time.

I look to Lochlin,* land of misty lakes,
 And there, along the billows swiftly blown,
Comes Fingal to Ithona's rocky shore,
 And few his heroes in this land unknown.

    * Lochlin, Scandinavia.

And Starno* sends to bid him to a feast,
   But Fingal thought of all the darksome past,
And how the king had Agandecca slain,
   And her sweet beauty to the breezes cast.

Then swift his anger rose, " Not Gormal's tower
   Nor Starno's self shall Fingal now behold ;
Let death brood o'er his quickly fleeting soul !
   Death be the shadow on his hearth-stone cold !

" Can I forget his daughter, beam of light,
   Whose life for mine was wasted by his hand ?
Go, son of Loda, say his words are winds
   Tossed to and fro across a dreary land.

" Here are my heroes from across the wave,
   They rise around me in this land unknown ;
Come round me, children, clash the shields afar,
   And tear false Starno from his rocky throne."

Around the king the warriors rise in wrath,
   No words come forth, they seize the ready spears ;
Each soul is inward rolled, and on each hill
   The wind the murmur of each war-song hears.

Then, eager for the fight, each clangs his shield,
   Comes Duthmaruno, hunter of the boar,
And Struthmor, dweller of the battle's wing,
   And Croma swift, whose ships seek every shore.

* Starno, a king of Lochlin.

But as wide bounding over Turthor's waves
   Rushed Fingal in his arms, a silver beam
Lit up the darkness of a glittering rock,
   Which raised its head above the curdling stream ;

And in the midst a stately form appears,
   A maiden white, her hair soft-floating wide,
Unequal are her steps, her white arms toss
   To her wild song across the surging tide.

      Look down, thou chief of Lulan, look
         From Loda's* misty Hall,
      While here from off my lonely rock
         I through the darkness call.

      I see thee sporting through the mist
         Along the nightly sky,
      The moon behind thine airy shield
         Doth oft in darkness lie.

      And kindled into meteors bright
         I see thy shining hair,
      Which sailing with the night along
         Are lost in morning air.

      But why am I forgotten here
         Upon my rock alone?
      Forgotten in my wind-swept cave,
         With winds to hear my moan?

            * Loda, Odin.

Then Fingal answered, "Voice of lonely night,
   Who art thou sighing o'er the dusky wave?"
She trembling heard, and then in fear she turned
   To hide within the darkness of her cave.

But Fingal loosed the thong from off her hands,
   And asked her of her father, till the maid
Returning to the moonlight of the rock,
   No more shrank from him in the night afraid.

     My father Torcul-torno dwelt
       By Lulan's foamy stream,
     But now he shakes the sounding shell
       In Hall where heroes dream.

     He met fierce Starno of Lochlin,
       Long fought the dark-eyed kings,
     And far across the stormy wave
       The noise of battle rings.

     My father Torcul-torno fell,—
       I chased the bounding deer,
     I heard a noise, and stayed my step
       To greet my father near ;—

     Only to see his bloody shield,
       And Starno's gathered smile ;
     He raised the sail, he bore me here,
       Lone to this rocky isle.

"Where is my father?" wild I cried;
　Dark waved his shaggy brow,
He showed the shield,—but, is there none
　To help me even now?

At times comes Starno like a mist,
　And holds before my eyes
My father's sword, his bloody shield,
　Till my hot tears arise;

But sometimes comes a beam of light,
　And hopes of life unroll,
For Swaran, son of Starno, dwells
　Within my lonely soul.

"Oh maid of Lulan, daughter of deep grief,
　As streaks of fire across a stormy cloud
Thy words roll o'er my heart, and in my ears
　The winds of passion call with voices loud.

"Look not for vengeance to the dark-robed moon,
　Look not to glancing meteor of the sky,
My gleaming steel thy sorrow shall surround,
　And soon on bloody field thy foes shall lie.

"Our maidens waste not in dark caves of streams,
　Nor toss their white arms to the dreary night,
But fair in Selma, o'er their sounding harps
　Fall the long streamers of their tresses bright."

Then raged the battle where the mighty kings
    Fought long beside the Turthor's foaming flood,
First Starno fell, then Swaran, beam of light,
    And low his golden hair was rolled in blood.

When rose the star of day from out the east,
    The yellow beam shot o'er the bright'ning tide,
But silent now the clash of shield and spear,
    Where heroes lie the mossy rocks beside.

And Fingal passed to where on sea-bound rock,
    Great Torcul-torno's daughter through the night
Had feared wild Starno, but with gleaming dawn
    Now watched for Swaran in the redd'ning light ;

And when from out her cave the white-armed maid
    Looked forth upon great Starno's bloody shield,
Her song arose for Torcul-torno gone,
    The song of Lulan echoed to the field ;

But when she saw the helmet cleft in twain
    Of Swaran in the beauty of his pride,
She shrank from Fingal, darkened all her face,
    And song of woe passed o'er the rolling tide ;—

      Art fallen by thy hundred streams
        Oh love of mournful maid,
      Called in the beauty of thy youth
        Like summer flower to fade.

THE MAID OF LULAN.

No more beside my lonely rock
    Shall I behold thee near,
No more like kindling star of hope
    Shall thy bright light appear.

I see Uthorno from the waves
    Rise high in clouds of night,
Upon whose steep and dusky sides
    Play meteors quick and bright ;

And there the misty Loda dwells,
    The house where heroes rest,
The spirits of the dead abide
    Upon thy shrouded breast ;

And there Cruth-Loda bends above,
    The parting mists between,
His right hand rests upon his shield,
    Half shrouded, and half seen ;

And in his left the sounding shell,
    And as from fields afar
The heroes come, he holds it forth
    To those who shone in war ;

But to the weak his shield is dark,
    And like a star that dies,
To feeble souls he sinks in mist
    Beyond the clouded skies.

THE MAID OF LULAN.

And there doth Torcul-torno sit
    Within the Hall of Shells,
And Starno, king of terror now,
    In Hall of Loda dwells.

But see advancing through the shades
    Young Swaran, golden beam,
And in his hand he takes the shell,
    And lightnings round him gleam.

And as the roof of Loda's Hall
    With nightly fire glows red,
And on my lonely rock look down
    The faces of the dead,

Amid the ridge of formless shades
    Will Swaran greet my sight,
And far to him my song shall rise
    Across the gloom of night.

STRINA-DONA.

Night sank upon the field
As horn of Fingal sounded on the wind,
And sons of wooded Albion returned
To Turthor's stream, and there the footsteps stayed,
For silent lay tall heroes in their blood
Beside the oozy wave.
    "Not harmless now
Returns my eagle from the field of foes,
O, chief of Crathmo-craula," cried the king;
" Rise in thy strength, here Fingal waits for thee!
Bold Duthmaruno, hunter of the boar."

But paled the mighty chieftain in his blood,
And low his voice beside the dusky stream—
" Like murmur of these waters came the race
Of wild Ithona down. Great Storno led
With Swaran of the stormy isles. They looked
From off their iron shields, all fiery-eyed,
Like to Cruth-Loda when he looks behind
The darkened moon, and strews his signs on night.

" We met by Turthor's stream ; like ridgy wave
We heaved and shook; the echoing strokes were mixed,
And shad'wy death flew swift across the hosts,
Who closed like showers of hail when squally winds
Catch in their trailing skirts.

     Nor harmless there
The fire of Duthmaruno's sword ; but now,—
Like ghosts of warriors gone, I pass ; for me
Shall wake no more the horn, the clash of arms,
Or Songs of Selma's halls."

     Then Fingal called
For harp of Ullin ; bade the song arise
To ease the warrior's soul to shades of death.
" No falling fire, seen but a moment's space,
Then lost in night ; no glancing meteor he
Now laid so low ; but like the strong-beamed sun,
Which shines for long rejoicing on his hill,
Was Duthmaruno, hunter of the boar !
Rise, harp of Ullin ! call his father's names
From their abode of old ! "

 Ithorno rising midst the ridgy sea,
  With head so gloomy in the sea-fog lost,
 From thy lone vales came forth a fearless race,
  And strong as eagle's young on tempest tossed.

 From thee came Colgorm of the iron shield,
  And Corcul-Suran mighty king of shells,

P

They came to woo fair Strina-Dona white,
   Where by the Cruruth's source the maiden dwells.

They came, strong sons of Loda's windy Hall,
   To Tormath's isle, where Luthan's streamy hill
Bends woody head above a dewy vale
   And murmuring waters the long echoes fill.

And there came heroes of the iron shields,
   And youths with heavy locks, to Rurmar's hall,
To woo the stately huntress of the wild,
   But Strina-Dona careless looked on all.

If on the heath she moved, her form was fair,
   And whiter was she than the cana-grass;
If on the sea-beat shore, the flying foam
   Did not on summer gale more lightly pass.

Her face was Heaven when seen through fleeting
     showers,
   Her eyes were stars of deep and steady light,
Her dark hair flowed around on stormy wind,
   And like a cloud, her soul was high and white.

Then in their ships from far Ithorno's shore,
   The mighty Colgorm, Corcul-Suran came,
The brothers from Ithorno, came to woo,
   Two moths to flicker round one torch's flame.

And Strina-Dona, from her streamy hill,
　　Saw them advancing in their echoing steel,
Her soul on blue-eyed Colgorm straight was fixed,
　　Nor did she strive her favour to conceal.

Wrathful the brothers frowned ; their flaming eyes
　　In angry silence met, then turned away ;
They struck their shields, caught fast their trembling
　　　　swords,
　　And rushed as foes into the bloody fray.

Strong Corcul-Suran fell, and on his isle
　　His father raged on far Ithorno's shore,
And from his home he turned bold Colgorm forth,
　　To wander on the winds for evermore ;

Till far on Crathmo-Craula's rocky field
　　He dwelt at length beside a foreign stream,
But not alone,—for Strina-Dona there
　　Shone ever as the glory of his dream.

So ceased the song of Strina-Dona white,
　　Then died in air the sound of Colgorm's name ;
But woke the thought of how from Colgorm's race
　　The chief of Crathmo, Duthmaruno, came.

　　　　Then ere he passed
The hero waked beside dark Turthor's stream,

And murmured low, " The deeds of other years
Are lights to dying eyes ! "
        Then past those lights
His spirit went like mist before the wind,
And night sank on the plain.

COLNA-DONA.

We came where Colna-Dona dwelt,
    The daughter of a king,
Her eyes were like the rolling stars,
    Her form what harp can sing?
Her smile a beam of sunshine bright,
Her soul a stream of golden light,
Her voice like breeze of summer night
    When the reed-warblers sing.

We came, three heroes from afar,
    To rear the tall white stone,
Where Fingal, son of Comhal, there,
    Strong foes had overthrown ;
Three bossy shields before us went,
Three bards above their harps were bent
To sing the fate of warriors, sent
    Upon the ghost-path lone.

I tore an oak from off the hill,
    And raised a flame on high,

I bade my father's shade look down
      From out the windy sky ;
I took a stone from out the stream,
Where sword of Fingal, silver beam,
Sent many a warrior's soul to dream
      Where reedy lakelets lie.

Beneath, I placed three bosses torn
      From off the shield of foes,
And in the earth a dagger keen
      And mail of steel repose ;
And round the stone we raised the mould
Beside the stream, where curdling cold
The blood of foes was tossed and rolled,
      Where the lone mound uprose.

And when from out the storm and mist
      Some traveller seeks its side,
The scream of the long trailing moss
      Shall in his ear abide ;
Battles shall rise around his head,
Blue-shielded kings, and swords blood red,
And darkened moon no radiance shed
      Above the crimson tide ;

And he shall burst from morning dreams,
      And from his scattered fears,
And ask, " Whence are these ghostly tombs ?
      This stone that lone appears ? "

And swift the aged shall reply,
" Here foes of Fingal silent lie,
And Ossian raised the mound on high
  To deeds of other years."

Then Carul came, the stranger's friend,*
  And bade to hall of kings ;
He brightened 'tween his aged locks
  As white as sea-gull's wings ;
While Colna-Dona, beam of light,
Shines through the blueness of the night,
And from amid the torches bright
  The harp of Crona rings ;

Till Carul thought of other days,—
  " Ye bring the times of old,
When by wide Clutha's winding wave
  The mist of battle rolled,
Or when in Selma's lighted hall
My eyes on fair Roscrana fall,
In vain the hound and hunter call,
  For dreams of love unfold."

Then sweet from Colna-Dona rose
  The song of war and love,
And Toscar darkened in his place
  The fields of slain above,—

* The stranger's friend, a host, one given to hospitality.

Till like a beam from waves that roll,
The beauty of the maiden stole
Across the passion of his soul,
    And fast his pulses move.

Pale grows the path of heroes passed,
    The troubled ghosts are laid,
As swift as when 'neath mounting sun
    The mists of morning fade ;
And love a fuller rapture brings,
His soul sweeps high on eagle's wings,
As flash across the sounding strings
    The white arms of the maid.

With morning light we waked the woods,
    And chased the path of roe,
They fell beside fair Crona's* stream,
    We marked their steps below ;
When from the wood with pointless spear,
And bloody shield, and face of fear,
And heavy step, see youth appear
    Who raised a tale of woe.

" Beside fair Crona's mossy stream
    Sweet Colna-Dona strayed,
But now in desert wastes afar
    Laments the lonely maid ;

---

* Crona, a tributary of the Carron.

A stranger came with morning bright,
He tracked the maiden's footsteps light,
And now as sinks the gloom of night
    She cries aloud for aid."

And Toscar heard : " Reach here thy shield,
    Marked thou the warrior's way ?
His strength shall fall, his head lie low,
    Ere dies the beam of day ;
Like meteor from a midnight sky,
Or wreath of spray when winds be high,
As riven cloud his ghost shall fly
    From out his bleeding clay."

He took the shield, his eyes rolled fierce,
    Then melted soft as morn
When o'er the calm and purple hills
    A summer day is born,—
For there were Colna-Dona's eyes,
And swift the maiden's blushes rise,
And though pale night fall from the skies,
    For love, it is but dawn.

Then glows the hall, the feast swells high,
    Then sounds the voice of song,
And Crona of the rippling wave
    Murmurs her rocks among ;

Praises of Colna-Dona bright,
And Toscar with his shield of might,
Pass on the breezes of the night
    To Selma's halls along.

THE WOOING OF EVERALLIN.

SHE comes from off the sunset hills,
    As here beside fair Cona's stream
The long past days of other years
    Come back to Ossian like a dream.

For oh, Malvina, white-armed maid,
    Sweet daughter of the hand of snow,
To me returns the ancient time,
    And songs forgotten long sing low.

My age is burdened down with grief,
    My sighs rise ghost-like on the wind,
But think not, daughter of the harp,
    That I was always mournful, blind.

My years have swift in battle rolled,
    Soon must I hold the sounding shell,
But bright the years of long ago
    When Everallin loved me well.

For me no day then passed its noon,
   And never was my heart forlorn,
In Everallin's golden smile
   Dark midnight turned to glorious morn.

Brown was her hair upon the breeze,
   Her eyes like April skies were blue,
Fair was her skin, like cana* white,
   Her voice soft as the falling dew.

A thousand suitors sought the maid,
   From all she turned with swift replies,
On Ossian only did she look,
   None else was graceful in her eyes.

I went, by Lego's sable surge
   I sought her father's echoing hall,
And Branno, friend of strangers, heard
   My suit, where soft the waters fall.

Twelve of my chiefs were standing round,
   The sons of Morven listening there,
"O Branno of the sounding mail,
   We come to woo thy daughter fair."

" From whence," he said, " these arms of steel?
   Not easy is the maid to win,
But where the sons of Erin fail
   Great Fingal's son may enter in ;

* Cana, cotton-grass.

" And though within my sounding hall
   Twelve beauteous daughters here were mine,
Since blest the maid who waits for thee,
   The choice should still be only thine."

Then to the maiden's bower we came,
   Joy kindled in each manly breast,
And every chief in Branno's hall
   The lovely Everallin blest.

Then on the further hill appeared
   Eight chiefs, with stately Cormac proud,
The heath shot lightnings from their arms,
   And spear and shield were clashing loud.

And eight were Ossian's heroes brave,
   And long and fierce the battle shook,
And spear and shield flew splintered wide,
   And redder ran the mossy brook.

Till Cormac's chiefs were laid full low,
   Till at my stroke the leader fell,
But Ossian only joyed because
   Fair Everallin loved me well.

O maiden with the sweet blue eyes,
   Whoever would have told me then,
That I, forlorn and sad, should end
   My journey through the paths of men.

That thou, my star, so soon would set,
  That night would settle on my noon,
And I should wander lone by day,
  Lone 'neath the changes of the moon.

Dark was thine hair, and blue thine eyes,
  Soon didst thou tread the dark'ning way,
I laid thee in thy narrow tomb
  And night had fallen on my day.

And sometimes from thy windy hill
  Thy shad'wy form would white appear,
And in the breezes of the night
  My soul has sometimes felt thee near,

And suns have burned, and suns have set,
  Yet Ossian sings forlorn, to tell
How in the days of other years
  Fair Everallin loved me well.

THE END.

www.ingramcontent.com/pod-product-compliance
Lightning Source LLC
Chambersburg PA
CBHW030313270326
41926CB00010B/1350